Hey Nature Lady

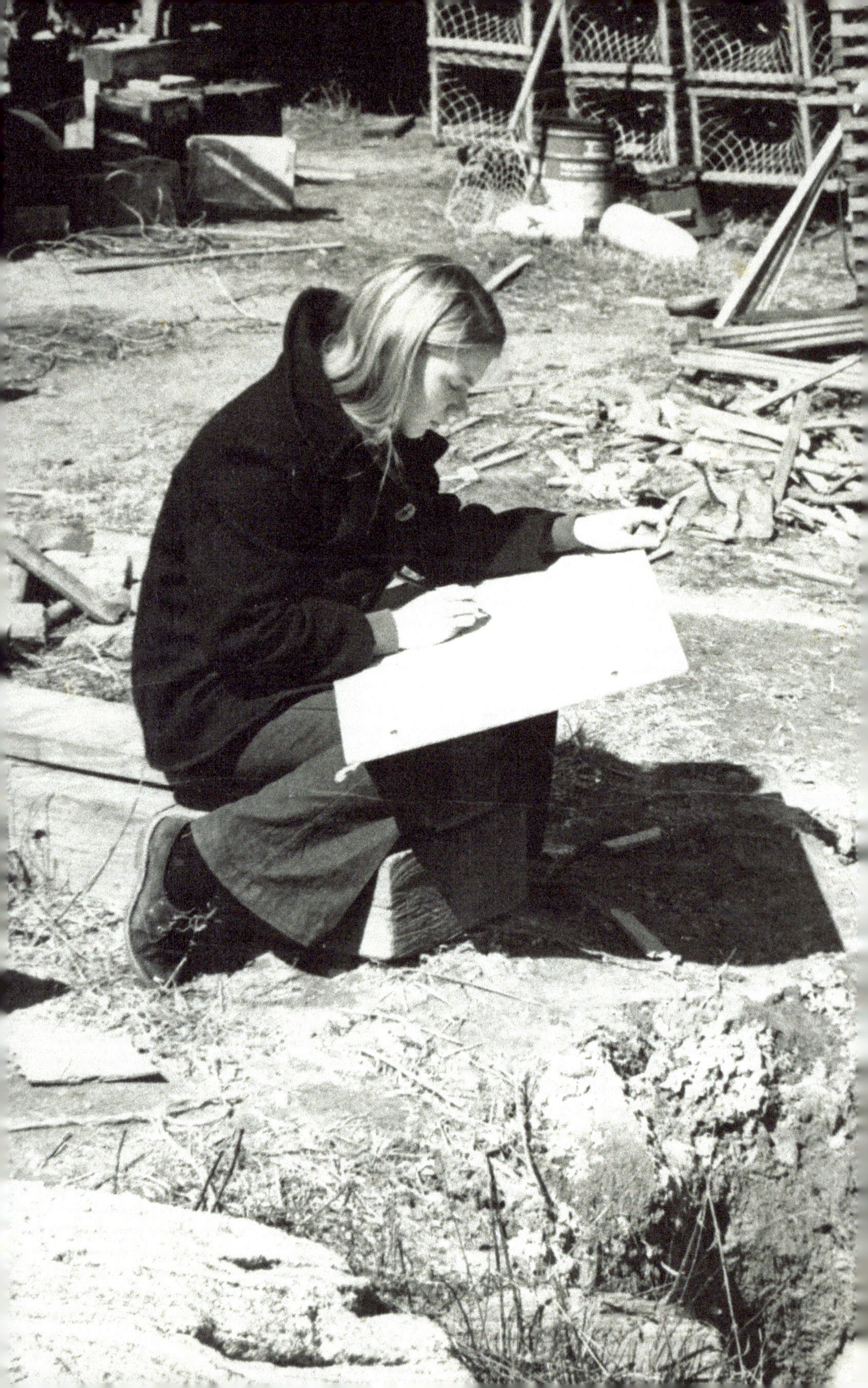

Hey Nature Lady

VIGNETTES ON LIVING A CREATIVE LIFE

Jane Howard

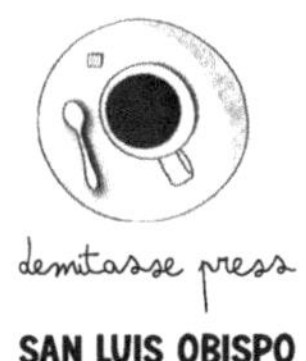

SAN LUIS OBISPO

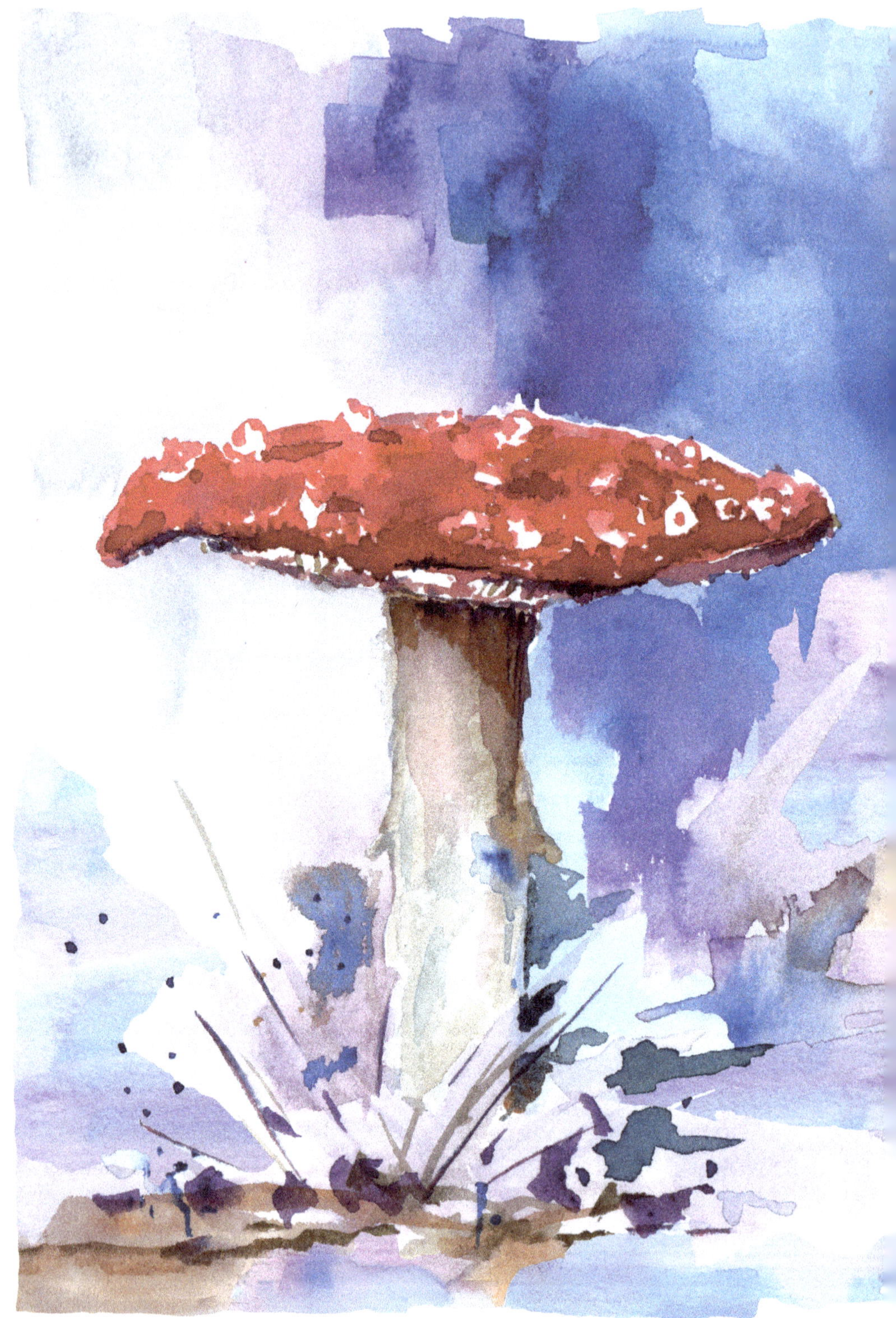

Amanita muscaria. A fabulous fairy-tale fungus. An exquisite toadstool. Its striking beauty involves white gills and a red cap (usually) with white spots. Known to be toxic, hallucinogenic, and medicinal, this delightful mushroom may appear one day and disappear the next. The wild *Amanita muscaria* has a relationship with the roots of pine trees, transferring nutrients into the tree's roots. In Germany and other parts of Europe, finding one of these gems is thought to bring good luck. *Muscaria* comes from the Latin word *musca,* meaning fly. Common name: fly agaric.

Hey Nature Lady: Vignettes on Living a Creative Life

ISBN paperback: 979-8-9929974-1-5

ISBN e-book: 979-8-9929974-2-2

ISBN hardcover: 979-8-9929974-0-8

ISBN hardcover Global Edition: 979-8-9929974-3-9

For permissions, inquiries, or more information, contact: info@islandjanejourneys.com

Cover and interior design by Dorka Hegedus

Book production by Demitasse Press

Printed in the United States of America, First Edition

Names: Howard, Jane (Jane Olivia), author.
Title: Hey Nature Lady : vignettes on living a creative life / by Jane Howard.
Description: First edition. | [San Luis Obispo, California] : Demitasse Press, [2025]
Identifiers: LCCN: 2025906081 | ISBN: 9798992997408 (hardcover) | 9798992997415 (paperback) | 9798992997422 (e-book)
Subjects: LCSH: Nature. | Ecology. | Nature stories. | Conservation of natural resources. | Wildlife conservation. | Environmental education. | Creative ability. | Environmentalism. | Travel--Anecdotes. | Ecoliterature. | Inspiration. | Perseverance (Ethics) | LCGFT: Essays. | BISAC: YOUNG ADULT NONFICTION / Science & Nature / Environmental Conservation & Protection. | NATURE / Essays. | TRAVEL / Essays & Travelogues.
Classification: LCC: QH81 .H68 2025 | DDC: 508--dc23

For all the creative spirits in my life

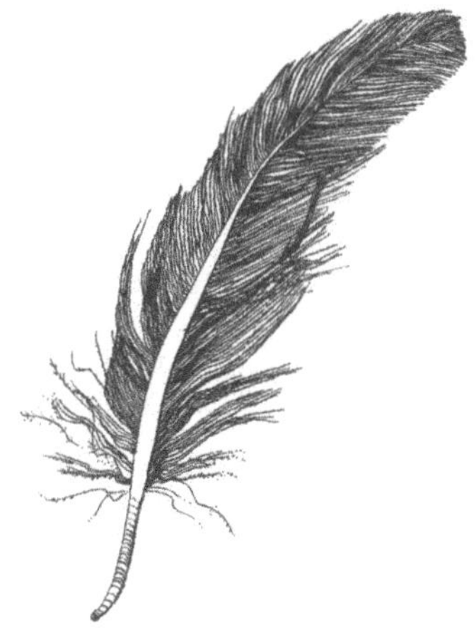

All artwork by Jane Howard, including transformative studies and creative interpretations.

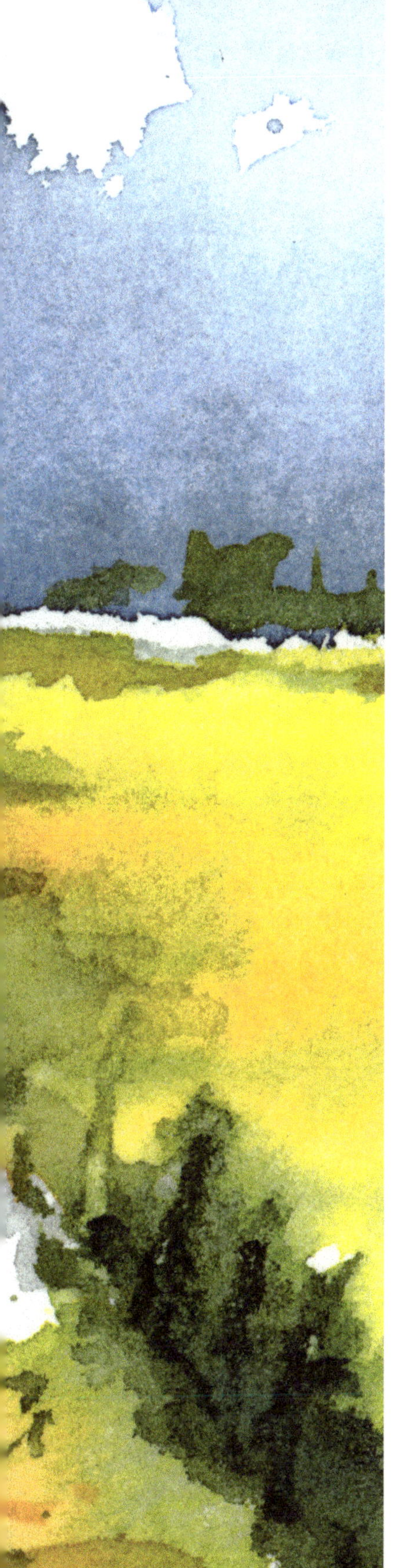

CONTENT

Hey Nature Lady

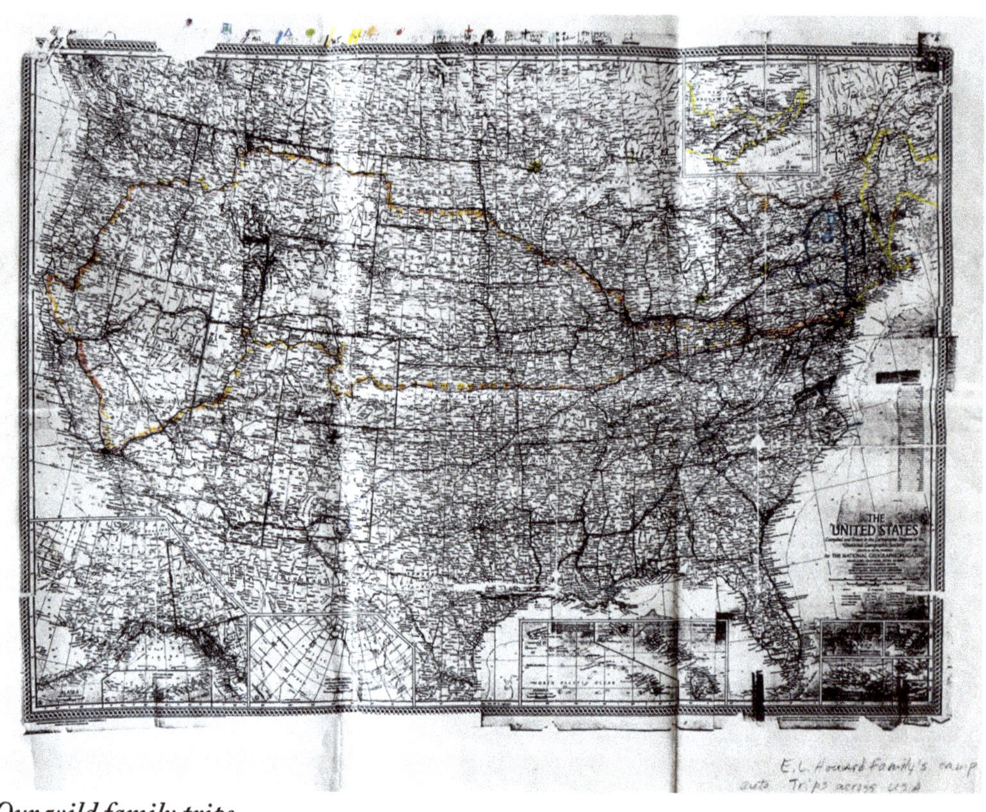

Our wild family trips

INTRODUCTION

I had the good fortune of visiting almost every national park in the United States in the early 1960s while still living under my parents' roof. A map taped to the wall behind our family's kitchen table charted our adventures. Each year, a new color of yarn was strung on the map between a pin marking our home outside New York City and a pin marking some believe-it-or-not place of natural wonder—our destination. The rear bumper of our Plymouth Fury station wagon sported a hand-drawn "California or Bust" sign, baffling gas attendants along the way.

My camp job back then was to blow up seven air mattresses, without a foot pump. My older sister helped Mom cook the camp stew, and my three brothers set up the tents and fetched water while Dad studied a map and made a fire. After chores, we wandered freely. You would've found me talking to the animals and trees, or using charcoal from our campfire to sketch stacked lobster traps.

"Life—a never-ending journey and you never get there," my Dad used to say. My brothers would tell me to stop asking so many questions, questions no one had answers for. So, I lived in my own world, a fascinating world wherein I discovered hummingbird nests in Nova Scotia, fed spunky chipmunks at the Grand Canyon, and stayed up all night to spy on the raccoons with clever hands that raided our Coleman coolers. I learned early on to respect nature's power—from nearly drowning in a powerful surf's undertow at Jones Beach, to being rescued from a flooding Blind River (formerly known as Blind Brook), to outrunning a violent tornado in Oklahoma, to encountering bold elk herds in Yosemite and charging bison in Yellowstone.

By the time I was too cool to car camp with my pioneering family of seven, I'd already become Nature Girl, well on my way to Nature Lady.

Hey Nature Lady is a collection of fun stories and original artwork inspired by some key experiences with nature and creativity. The essays are loosely chronological, moving from when I was a bright-eyed innocent just out of college intent on changing the world to later years as I built a teaching career, first in public and charter schools and ultimately in outdoor schools that I chose to create. Memory is a mysterious mechanism—it can be selective, and it sometimes distorts history. I recorded the stories in this book from my own memory, keenly aware that my own interpretation may not always match how others experienced the same events. I trust that readers will receive these stories in the playful spirit in which I wrote them.

I invite readers to notice nature's gems and infinite magic for themselves, to follow their own journey of creativity and self-discovery, and to continue the important traditions of environmental education: Awareness, Sensitivity, Knowledge, and Understanding.

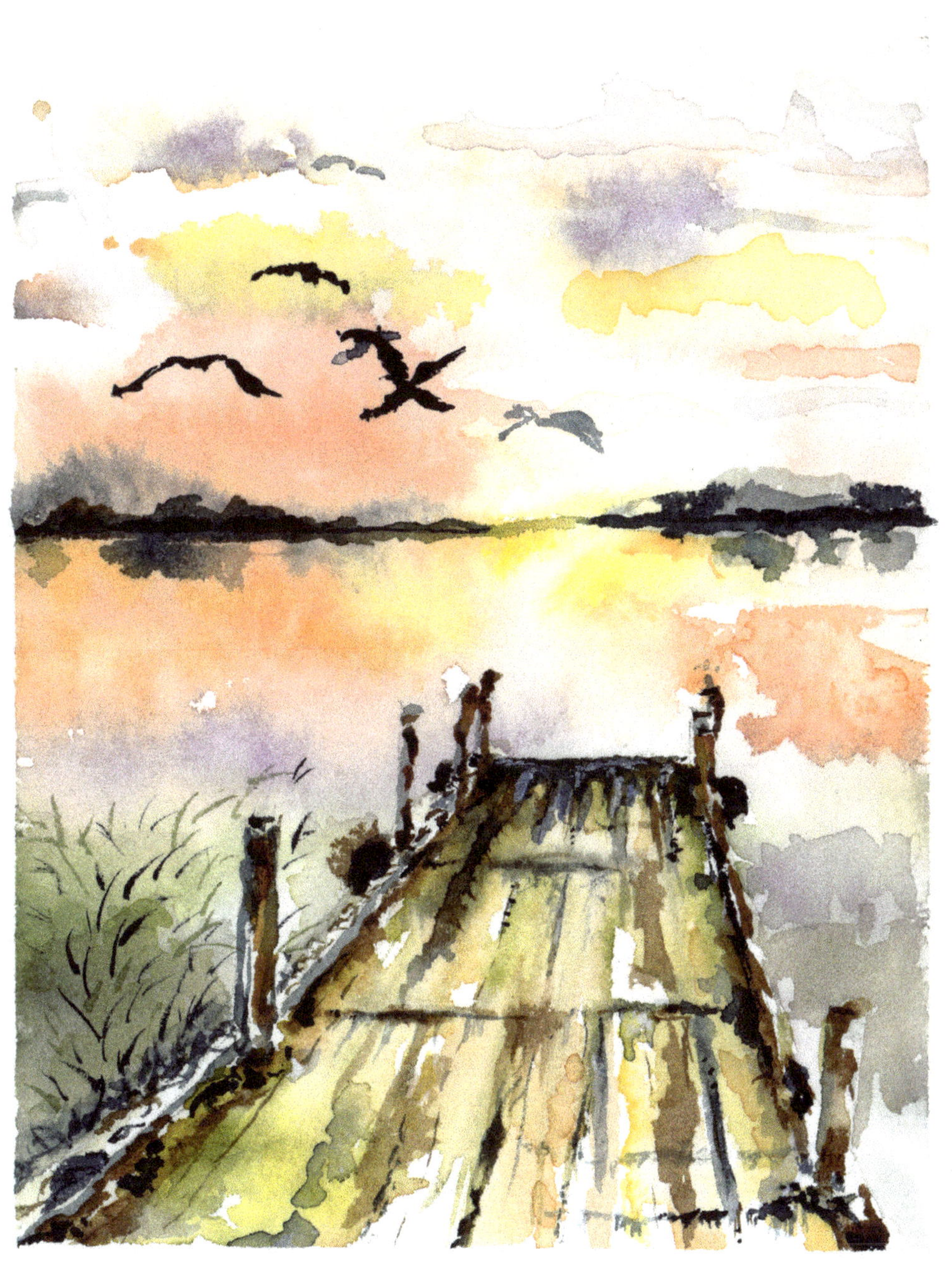

Chapter 1

A Slight Delay

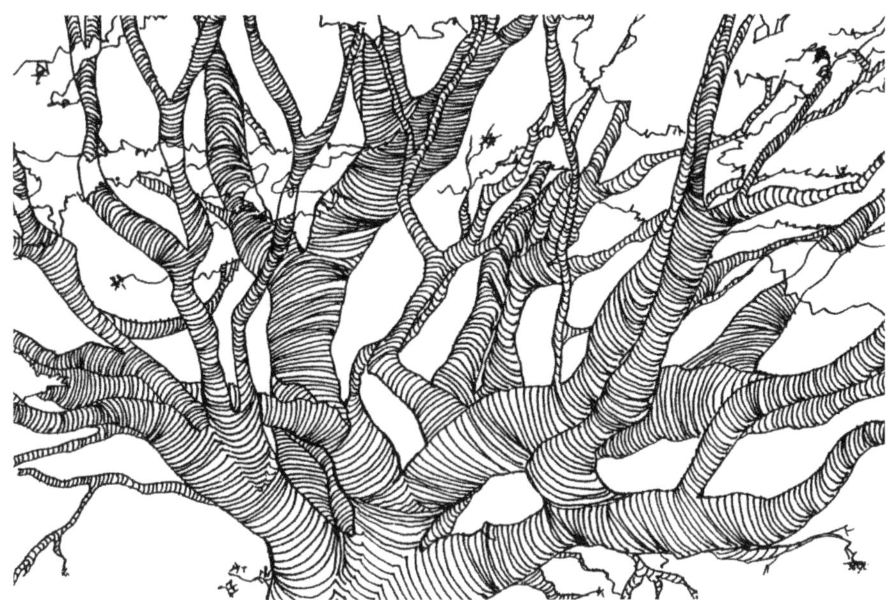

I shoved through the resistance of the closing door to enter a slowly moving northbound train. Just behind me, an older guy who'd been sprinting to catch the train squeezed through the same door. He deposited his sweat-soaked body with exaggerated effort into a seat facing mine across the main aisle. The train was crowded and smelled like stagnant cigars. The air conditioning must have been out of service. I sat clutching my books, feeling lucky to have caught this rapidly accelerating train departing Grand Central Station on a sweltering summer's eve. The year was 1975. I was a fresh-eyed college student returning from acing a dream-job interview in New York City and ready to save the world.

I must've dozed off in the heat but managed to hear a distant muffled voice make the routine call. "Next stop, Rye. Rye train next. All stops to Rye. Next stop Rye. Ryyyyye. All tickets, please. All tickets," rang throughout the car, along with the sound of tickets being punched. The conductor asked me for $2.40 and continued to weave down the aisle, trailing the fading jingle of his belt change machine.

Suddenly, the train jerked and screeched to a halt. Another conductor appeared through the heavy sliding door separating the train cars. "Ladies and Gentlemen, there will be a slight delay," he called out. "We have a broken power shoe in our first car. We will be underway as soon as possible."

Taking the train to and from Grand Central Station was an exceptional treat for me, and on the ride into the city that morning I'd visualized how this summer job would lead to a future dynamite career. I spent the day interviewing at one of the "greenest" companies on the East Coast, and I felt positively on top of the world afterward. Both while coming and going from the city, my mind swam with ideas and possibilities. On this return trip, however, imagining my future commute, I did wonder whether such holdups happened often. My hometown was only about twenty-five miles from the city, but with delays the typical forty-five-minute train ride could feel like eternity.

As if the dripping man who'd boarded the train behind me could read my mind, he blurted out in exasperation and disgust to no one and everyone, "These delays happen at least once a week and always when it's hot and crowded! Gee, you take the train to avoid driving at the mercy of eight million other maniacs on the road."

"Just look at FDR Drive from the East River at rush hour," he snarled and continued his pontification. "It's the biggest parking lot in the world. On the train you're at the mercy of the charlatans who run this mess. The only answer is to take a helicopter—yeh, right. Trying to beat this commuting trap is major impossible."

While the snarky guy worked up a lather, I thought about my career goals. I thought about how I wanted to use my impending degree in Environmental Sciences to make positive changes in the world. I believed getting a meaningful job in the Big Apple would be a great way to apply my skills and focus in a purposeful manner.

Being my extroverted self, I decided to ask the loud, grouchy, not-that-old man why he didn't just live in the city or, better yet, why he didn't find a job where he lived and avoid a commute altogether. He chuckled at my sarcasm and carried on. "You know another thing, nobody ever talks to each other on these trains unless something like this is going on. It's sick that people never communicate unless they're forced to. You've heard of the New York gaze, right? Iceberg . . . makes us all feel cold and transparent. We're all on our own little tracks. I feel like I must have the plague, trying to get a smile returned with a smile from a stranger."

At this juncture, I smiled to myself and vowed never to fall off my own track of optimism and onto the tracks of this obsessive ranter who apparently carried some heavy baggage. During that slight delay, I promised myself I would strive to travel light and smile throughout life.

At an oppressively stale moment, the man leaned his scrunched, red face into the center aisle. "Let me tell you something," he seethed. "Only a few years ago I was like YOU. I had just finished school and come to New York. I thought everyone was going to be cool. Well, it isn't exactly a field of daisies, you know. People grow up here with hate and prejudice. I'm being realistic."

At this point, I shifted my posture and disengaged from this toxic downside lecturer, wishing the train would start moving. I didn't want to hear any more for fear he'd infect my idealism.

"You can't change the minds of huge groups of people," the man snorted.

Then, he spotted my previous semester's textbook in my lap, *Introduction to Quantitative Analysis*. "Hey, and you can't quantitatively analyze people, man. Until people can empathize with their brother, there's no hope!" he cried out.

I sat back with a deep sigh, regretting that I'd entertained his diatribe. With his neck muscles now bulging, he went on to share that he'd gone to school, too. He'd felt close to learning something and becoming a free-thinking person while in college. But the reality of the almighty buck had driven him to give up on ideals.

"There's work to be done in this country," he emphasized while pointing at me. "What are young people like YOU doing to contribute?"

Just then, I was relieved to feel a slight jerk and the movement of hot air. I averted my eyes to focus on the world outside the train's grimy window. The conductor entered our car to proclaim the shoe repaired. A double toot sounded, and he finished his announcement through a broad smile. We would be underway immediately.

Forty-something years later, I look back with gratitude at that train ride and uncomfortable chance meeting. There was a slight delay on that hot summer evening, and not only with the train. I was exposed to the opinion of a person on a track opposite to the track I was on, and that left me with an impression and a cause for pause. There was a message in the meeting, one that prompted me to vow never to let downside thinking knock me over like a surprise wave at the beach, nor to let one person's negativism derail my personal goals and growth.

Nearing retirement, I now understand how that slight delay later helped me overcome many of life's obstacles and doubts and guided me toward fulfillment. That stuck train and the stuck man fueled the grit that got me through many years of self-nurturing and self-coaching—skills necessary to keep me on a happy track. Over the years that followed, I experienced countless rejection letters, job refusals, and lay-offs, and each time I got better at designing my own way forward. I've learned to recognize life's potential derailments and to remain resilient when wrecks do occur.

I remind myself my train is on the move. All aboard!

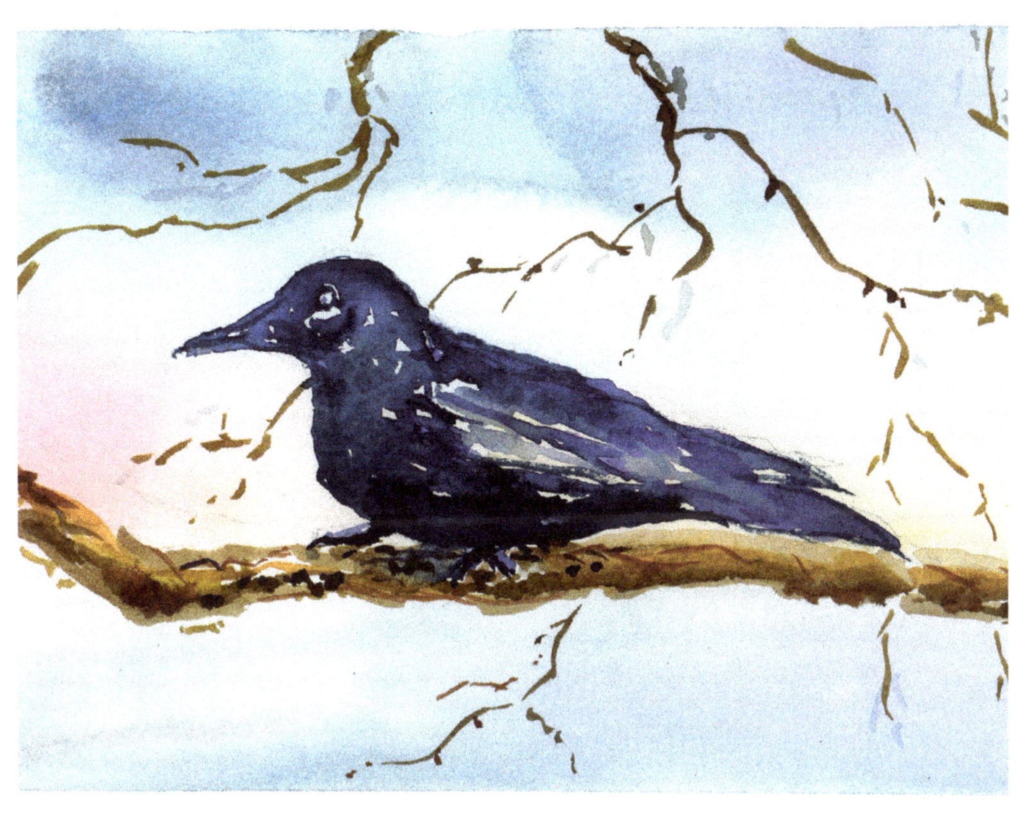

Chapter 2

Hey Nature Lady

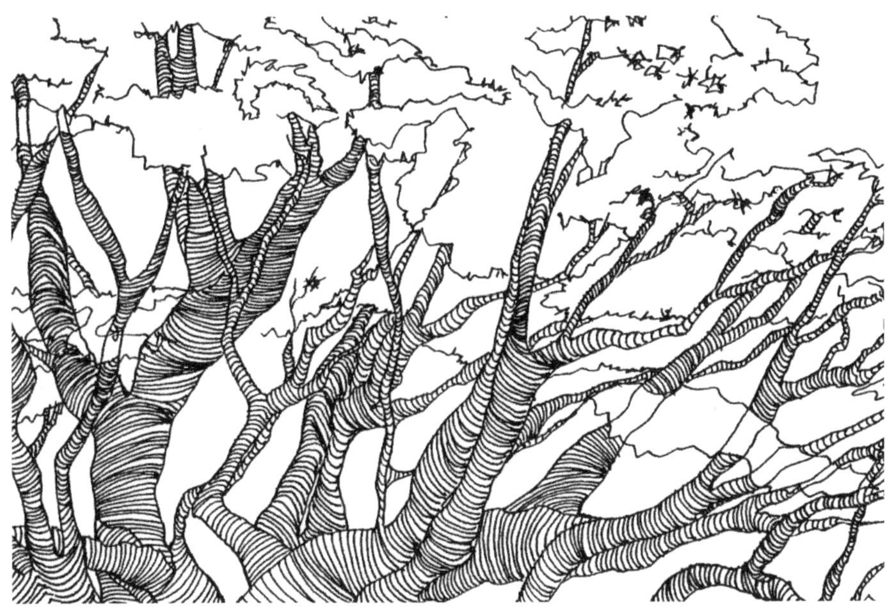

"Welcome to Camp New Horizons!" we shouted as the school bus pulled up to the central lodge at noon. I was happy not to have taken the summer "dream job" in New York City and excited to be a staff member at this seasonal outdoor school in the woods roughly one hundred miles north of the city. I'd been assigned to share my newly polished understanding and appreciation of nature—right up my alley. Having happily left behind the anxiety of urban life, I was at home in the woods. I seriously and purposely believed that being immersed for three nights in the damp northeastern pine woods, inhaling fresh mountain air, would provide our teenage campers with their greatest teacher. That had been true for me at their age.

As our fresh lot of fourteen-year-old campers sauntered off the bus, however, it was painfully obvious that making a difference with this group of inner city kids was going to be tricky. They had a brash vibe and looked cocky, ready for a fight, like they had their own ideas about how their three days in the woods would unfold. The first night was surprisingly straightforward. The transitions between icebreaker games, cabin assignments, unpacking duffel bags, lodge routines, and lights out protocols went as expected, and at least the staff got a good night's rest.

This was our third group of the summer, and over the prior two I'd fashioned a morning routine. Before the camp was alive with the buzz of operations, I would grab my camera and walk the Pond Trail to capture special nature moments in the early blue light. My nature photos hung in the lodge. I was especially proud of a macro print of green lichen with red, cup-like stalks popping out of a striated rock pounded smooth by years of rain. A blue award ribbon hung from my photograph of a faint morning shadow casting crepuscular rays on a dead, twisted, sun-bleached branch.

It wasn't until later that first morning that our camp director noticed the maintenance locker had been broken into. I didn't learn about the incident right away, as I was out on a trail with Bird Man, our resident ornithologist, who was guiding an early morning group. We tasked each camper with keeping a journal and recording what they observed. No one was looking at birds, though.

"Hey, Bird Guy, why don't you check out the nature trail?" several of the boys chanted.

The ornithologist and I turned to see that a transformation had occurred among the birch and the pines. Every tree was artistically showered with color. The naturally tranquil green and brown hues of the northeastern woods had been horrifyingly splattered with the dayglow markings of the spray paint that had been stolen from the camp supply locker. Bird Man gasped in shock. I stood by, disoriented. The kids had tagged the trees with graffiti that appeared as scrambled and confused as my dampened enthusiasm. So much for exposing urban teenagers to the wonders of nature.

Early on the second day as I walked to the lodge for breakfast, a towering, extremely buff, tough-skinned fourteen-year-old named Zion caught up to me, trailed by a pack of his equally rough-looking peers. Zion stepped directly into my path, and his bros created a wall, blocking my stride. They meant, and succeeded, to challenge and alarm me, but I kept my cool, at least outwardly. I stepped aside, heart pounding, and continued my pace with a fake half-smile.

I was rapidly and fully realizing the disconnect between our minimally trained staff and these urban kids. At breakfast, I watched Zion swagger about with his black, oversized, baggy pants hanging below his waist, revealing his butt crack. He positioned himself as "the man," strutting like a cocky rooster between the rows of campers and pancakes. He was clearly proud of his forest "artwork." I tried to imagine how he managed to keep his extremely white sneakers so clean.

We needed to have a staff meeting and take back control. But how? How was "Nature 101," my name for this new three-day program with the mission of exposing inner city youth to the natural world, supposed to work amidst a clash of paradigms? I contemplated this while on a solitary walk as I snapped a few photos of the variegated leaves underfoot and surprised myself by feeling some fleeting compassion salted with hope. These kids were just trying to blend in, to feel comfortable in an uncomfortable and unfamiliar environment. *They're only bringing their unique city style to the woods*, I heard my naïve, optimistic self-talk say.

I purposely avoided breakfast on the third and last day of "Camp Run-Amuck." That's the nickname the discouraged staff had bestowed on the camp because everything was running amuck. Zion and his "homies" had successfully intimidated most of the international staff and upset the incompetent camp director, who had disappeared into a self-destructive drinking spree, dosing himself with liquid medicine. Avoiding the lodge at breakfast would save me from the chaos of newly broken chairs and the cacophony of banging plates. As I walked alone, taking long, deep breaths, my thoughts drifted away from the mess of this program. I imagined becoming a park ranger or a classroom teacher instead.

Suddenly, rounding the corner of the first set of cabins, I almost collided with the lead man himself, who'd been tracking me. This time Zion was alone. Without an audience to impress, his voice was lower and softer, though still snide. "Hey, Nature Lady," he chided. "Why don't you check out the nature trail?"

Campers had been instructed to pack up for their departure and the three-hour return bus ride to the city, but Zion clearly wanted to show me something. In a moment of renewed hope, I imagined I'd made a slight difference in one young boy's life. When he pointed to the Pond Trail, my gaze followed. I froze, stunned. Overhead was strung a lanyard of frogs dangling by individual nooses. Some were still wriggling. My mouth hung open like a largemouth bass. Closing my eyes, I tried to erase the horrifying image of swinging amphibians. The school bus's abrasive and repeated horn blasts sounded departure time. I turned on my heels and sprinted to the lodge, feeling nauseated. I never did say anything to Zion.

My educational ideals were shattered. I felt numb, defeated, and helpless. Had this nature camp been a sham? Why hadn't we been appropriately trained? Had the mission of introducing inner city youth to the woods been recklessly idealistic?

As the teens gathered to board the bus, I picked up a forgotten football and whipped an anger-relieving pass across the lawn. Latisha, one of the campers, intercepted the ball from where it landed on the grass. Then, through the chaos of the crowd, someone yelled, "Hey, Latisha, stop! Get off. That grass is alive!"

It was Zion. He repeated his command in earnest. He pointed to Latisha's feet and yelled again, "Stop! Get off! You're stepping on it. You're killing it. Don't step on it. Seriously, didn't you learn anything here at camp? Grass is alive!"

Adolescence is a war, but as if to celebrate a winning team, the entire group broke out in intense chanting, dancing, and prancing on tiptoes. "It's alive! It's alive! It's alive!" "

Zion was last to board the bus, and he did so with a nod and a raise of his fist. After their outrageous vandalism and violation of nature, perhaps there was a singular takeaway for Zion and the challenging collective of campers. Shutting out the noise, I quietly hoped and wondered at the same time: Had one small connection with nature been made? I turned to a staff member and mumbled, "I guess we're learning as we go."

"Maybe three days in the woods will dissolve into something greater," she whispered back as the rowdy busload blew down the dirt road.

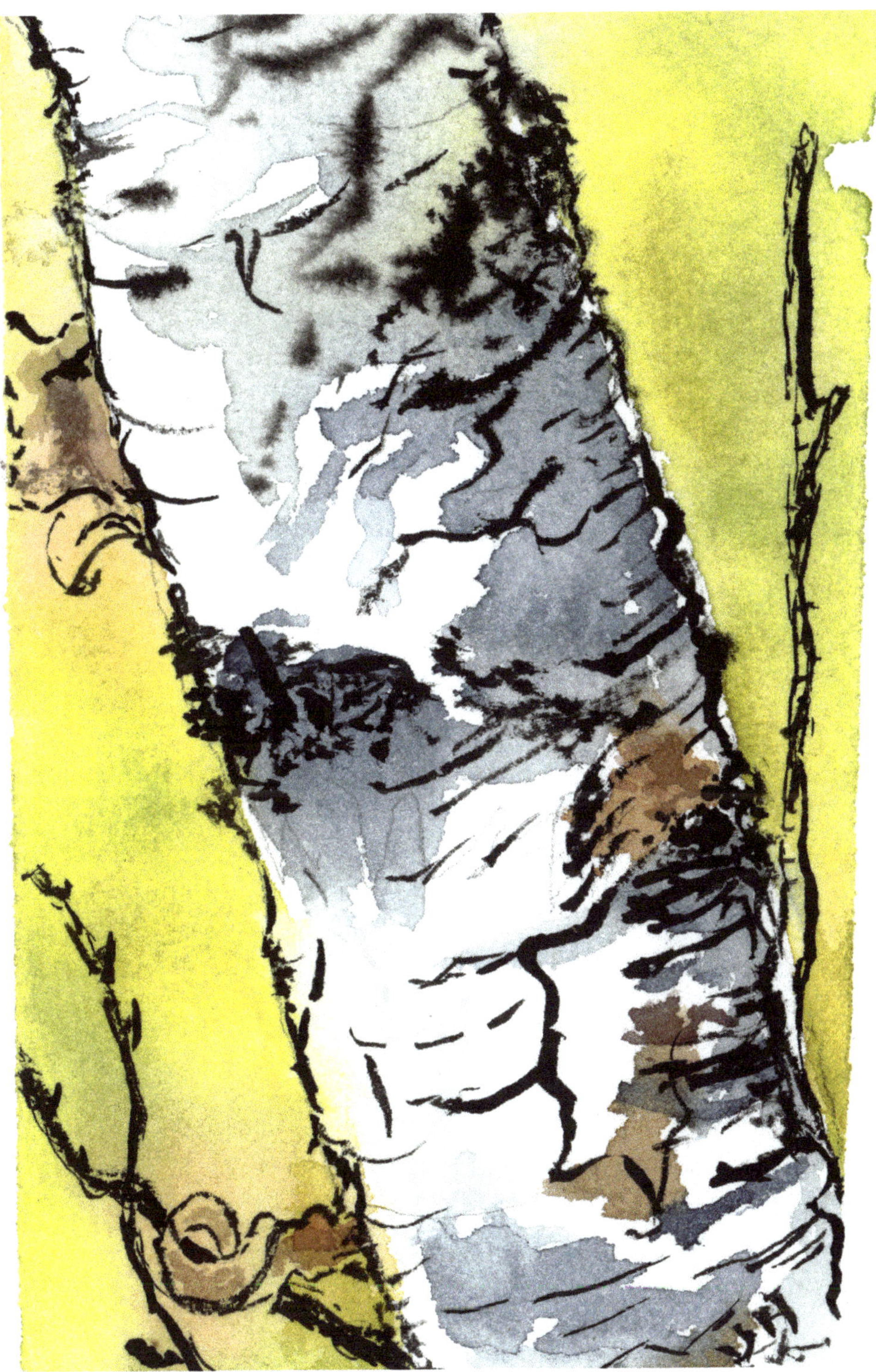

Addendum: Post-camp interview with Zion

As is customary with most educational programs, pre- and post-surveys were conducted to assess the merits of the "Nature 101" program.

Teacher: Zion, had you ever been to a forest before outdoor school?

Zion: No, and let me tell you about my experience with a pumpkin. A teacher gave it to me at school when I was eight. It was orange, sort of round but imperfect. It had dents and marks with many vertical lines running down from the center. It wasn't exactly smooth. Where is the plug? Where are the seams? I stood there with this giant pumpkin searching for the hole where the factory had squirted in all the gook. I asked the teacher how the factory workers got all the gooey stuff inside, but she shrugged me off. I had no clue that pumpkins—or trees—grew from a seed and that pumpkins are alive and can be food.

Teacher: What are your thoughts about nature?

Zion: I was told that rats the size of humans grew and thrived in the sewers of New York City. My friends called sidewalks "the floor." Wild places were far away, removed, and formidable. Nature meant things that creep and crawl and were to be eliminated. Not much was considered sacred.

Teacher: What do you remember learning at outdoor school?

Zion: I learned that grass is alive. But, hey, why does outdoor school have to be outdoors?

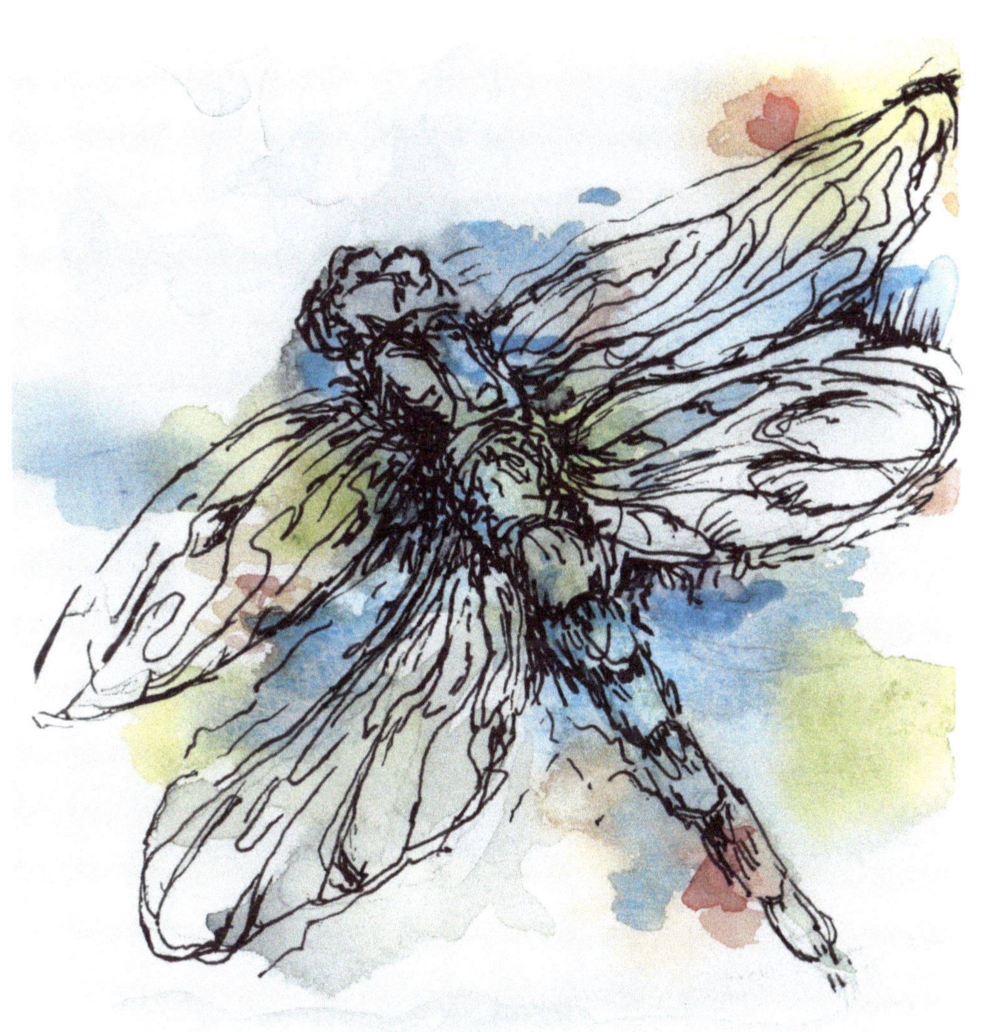

Chapter 3

Getting to School

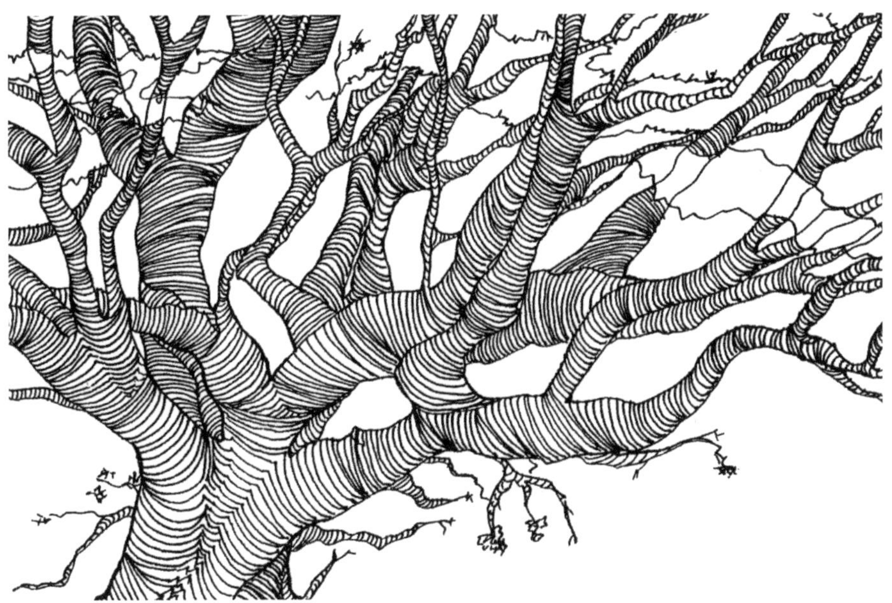

Attending art school in Central Mexico in 1973 was a fluke. I'd applied for an off-campus study in Europe, but going overseas was out of my grade-point reach. Alternatively, I was planted in the colorful, dusty Mexican town of San Miguel de Allende. I was excited for the adventure; it would certainly be better than spending another freezing, wet winter in the cornfields of Ohio, where I was a student at Ohio Wesleyan University.

Today, San Miguel is an artsy, colonial town and a UNESCO World Heritage site with an exploding expat community. In the 1970s, though, I was challenged to make my way to and from school each day. Most days I walked an odiferous mile between cornfields and open sewers, stumbling on uneven cobblestones while practicing my hola's and the few words of Spanish I picked up enroute. The warm air smelled like burning tortillas and rotting fruit. Barking dogs provided an incessantly noisy background. By the time I'd navigated the mile walk to school, I was exhausted.

One frightful, moonless night when walking home late, I rounded a curve on a rugged, wall-lined, dirt street named Calle Cri Cri and encountered a pack of savage wild dogs. The ferocious, foaming pack stretched from one wall to the other in an approaching phalanx. I could go neither forward nor around them. Broken glass bottles topped the entire length of the looming walls on either side of me, making them impossible to scale. My heart sank as I considered turning to run away from the growling dogs' dark shadows, picturing my backside being ripped apart. There was nowhere to flee. I was penned in, trapped. I held my breath and froze.

Then, zap! It hit me. *Be bold.* As I'd been coached by my Forest Service boss to do during bear encounters in the wilds of Alaska, I took on a stance of looking as large as I could imagine, rising on my toes, waving my arms, and shouting with a crazy-deep voice I didn't recognize. Reaching down, I grabbed a melon-size rock and hurled it as hard as I could at the pack. I missed, but the action broke up the line of beasts and managed to divide the leader from the followers, sending them all scattering. My heart hammered in my ears. *Wow, where did that courage come from?* I wondered.

Wild dogs, banditos, and other unwelcome surprises weighed heavily on my mind each day as I contemplated my laggard and imposing daily commute to and from school. I thought about the many children around the world for whom getting to school was a long and incredibly dangerous foot journey involving crossing rivers with ropes and pulleys, traversing perilous trails, or scaling high snow fields. But getting to school was a path to a better life for them, as it was for me. I needed to figure this out.

With my morale thin, I seized the opportunity to purchase an ancient easy-keeper horse from my landlord for a few pesos, postponing the animal's inevitable departure to the meat market. Pancho, which translates to "free," was more burro than horse. His way of life was dozing. He hung out untethered in the cacti in the scrubby vacant lot next to my casita and only reluctantly woke up when I prodded him the mile uptown with me on board. Once at school, Pancho would hang his old head afternoon-siesta-style for the next four hours, reins dragging in the dust. Pancho freed me from the fear of not getting to school safely, but only temporarily. A week after our meeting, I found his tired and worn-out old self dead in the neglected lot next to the casita.

Waking up late for class one day, I pleaded with my overgrown frat boy housemate to drive me to school. He gave a partied-too-hard-last-night grunt and surprised me by tossing over the keys to his tiny blue convertible. I was certain I'd mastered the getting-to-school challenge now. Going by car would certainly be speedier than by Pancho or walking. Jumping into the sporty Miata with its worn shocks, I rattled and bumped my way up the narrow Calle El Centro, which translates to

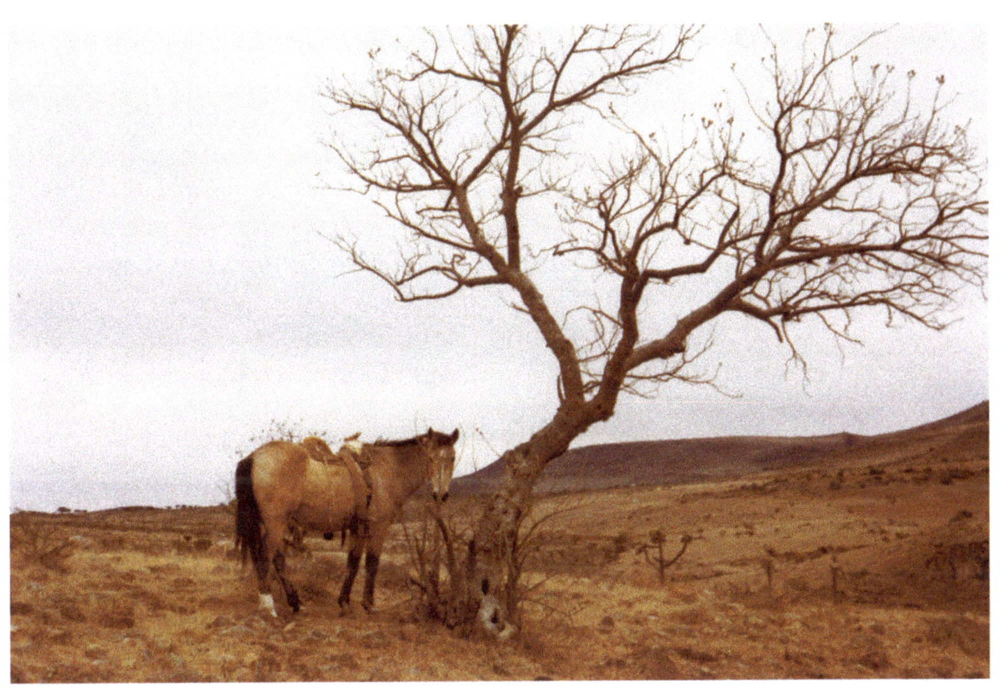

Pancho

"street going into the center of town." Unaware that all Centro streets are one-way streets, I passed the impressive church and directly in front of the police station going the wrong way.

Instantaneously, four uniformed Federales jumped into the road, yelling at me in Spanish. All four of them threw themselves on the hood of the convertible with a thud, shouting into my face, "Alto! Alto!" I wasn't fluent in Spanish, and certainly not in traffic terms, but I understood they wanted me to stop. Still, I didn't stop. Unaccustomed to the car and its stick shift, I hit the brake without depressing the clutch. The car lurched forward, sending the men in uniform tumbling to the street, which is most likely why I was escorted into the jailhouse.

Not fully understanding Spanish didn't stop me from realizing I'd been arrested and detained. Entrapment is a terrible, helpless condition. I wanted to flee, but I was stuck in a grimy cell where I sat solo on a bare, pee-soaked floor while four policia ignored me in favor of their game of dominoes. Hours seemed like days, and I sank into despair. I'd heard stories of people never getting out of a Mexican jail, and there I was—possibly never getting to school nor out of jail.

Fear was my true prison that day. At least until some force from deep within me suddenly sounded an internal alarm, zapping me with a burst of energy and guidance, and jolting me to seize the moment to meet the obstacle head-on. An inner voice spoke to me: *You've been stuck in predicaments before without an escape, so make a plan.* I'd arrived in Mexico with an open mind, and now I was going to learn to use my voice.

"Amigos!" I bellowed. "Quieres pesos?" You want pesos? I was working on a bribe.

One hundred pesos was a lot of money for me at the time, but—bingo!—it earned me a single landline phone call to my wild-thing housemate. While awaiting my housemate's long-after-dark arrival, I contemplated how the challenges I encountered in getting to school *were* my school, my education. I'd been tested day and night and learned how to source my own native power. I'd learned to take chances, to take risks. I'd learned to think and believe, to be creative and resourceful, to choose and focus on a strategy, to make a plan, and to follow through. I'd discovered the value of freedom and learned to hang onto the belief that a positive outcome was possible.

I'd also learned that any quantity of pesos is worth its weight in gold to escape a Mexican jail.

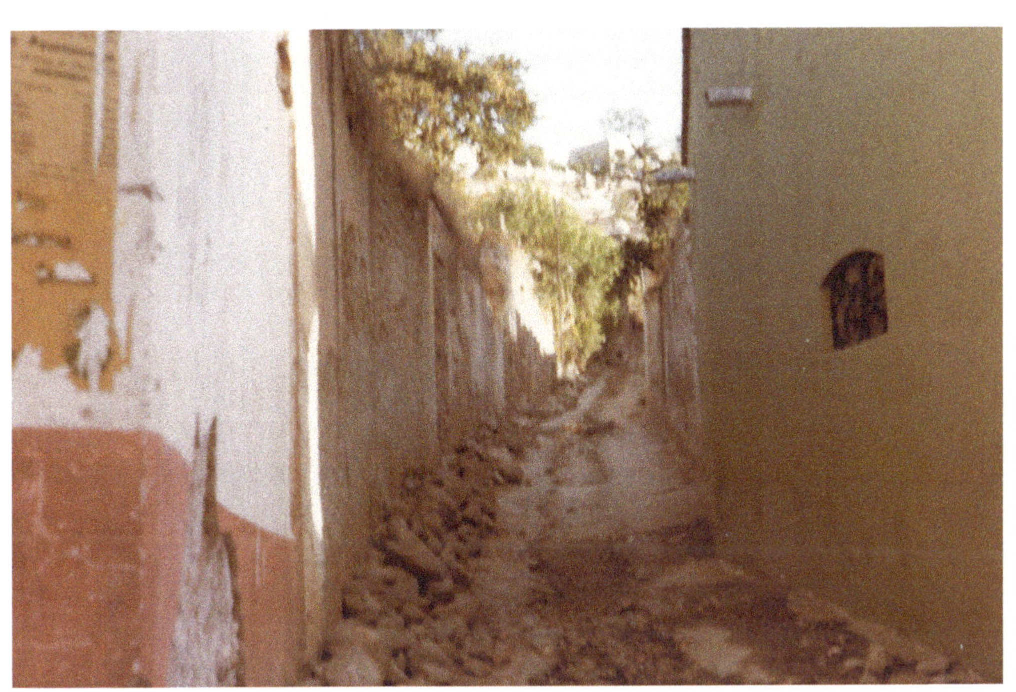

Calle Cri Cri

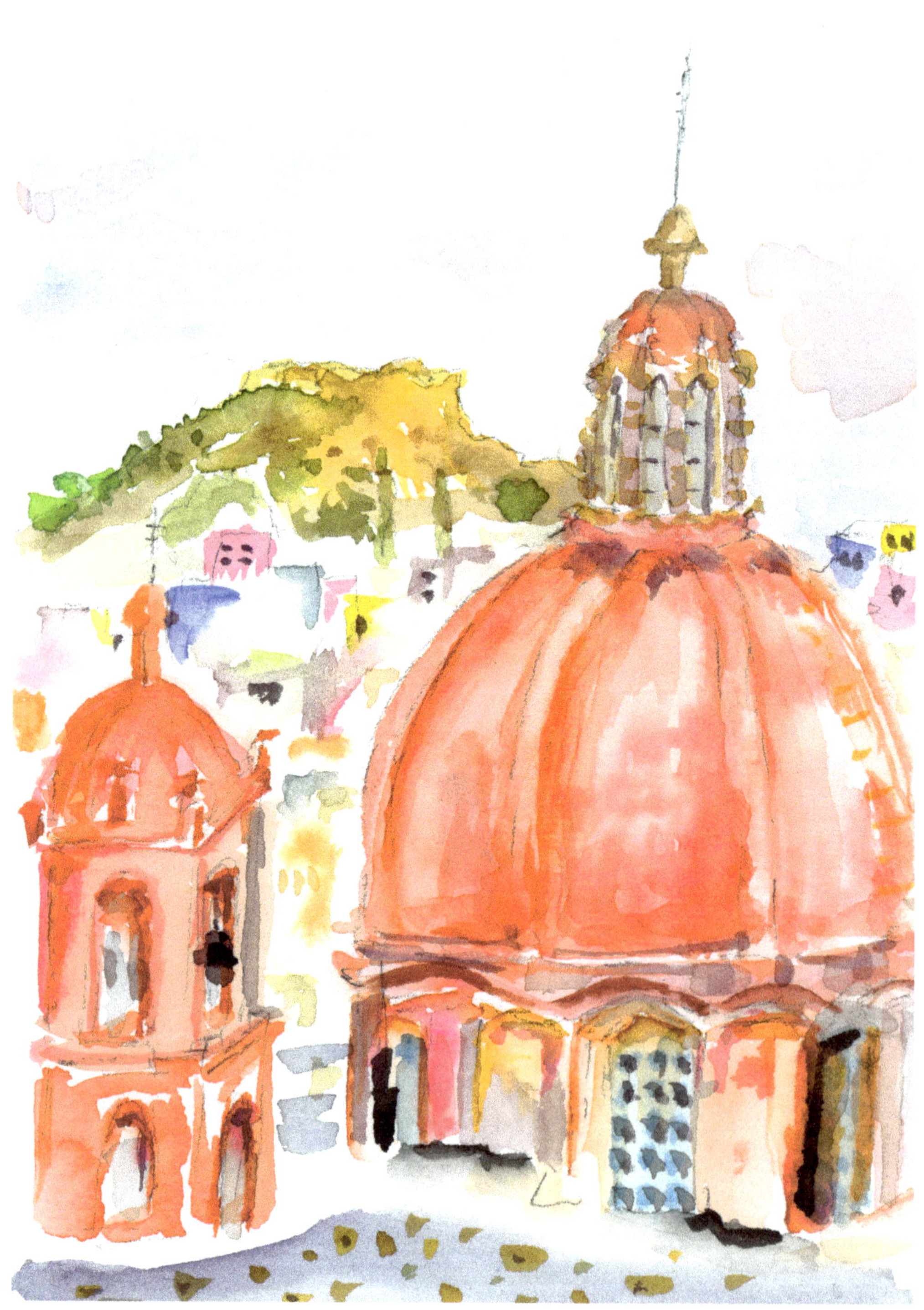

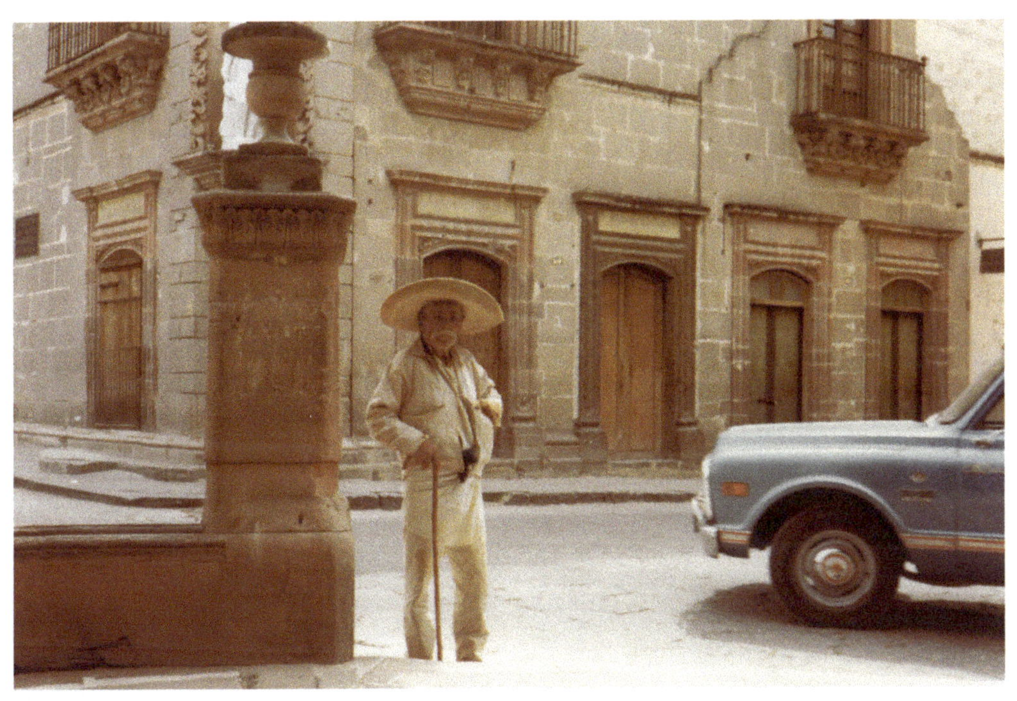

The landlord

Chapter 4

Wild Hearts

A TRIBUTE TO FUZZY

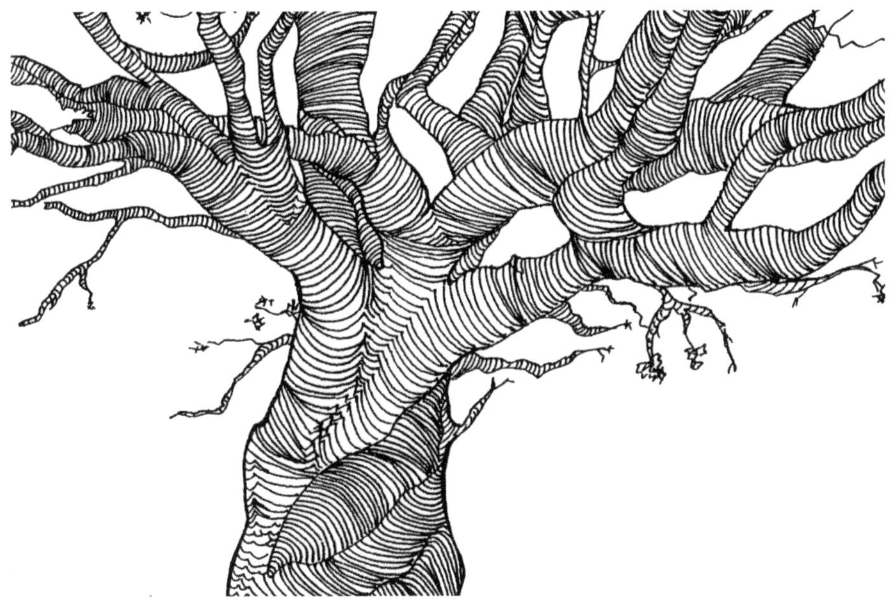

I woke to bits of moss and lichen littered on my face. Flat on my back with eyes suddenly wide open, I watched pieces of subarctic duff descend from cracks in the walls like gentle spitting rain. In the light of dawn, a confetti of forest debris was dusting my sleeping bag while our tiny driftwood shelter inexplicably oscillated from side to side. Holding my breath, I lay prone and motionless on a hard wooden plank, consumed by dreadful racing thoughts. Suddenly, a big chunk of moss popped out of one of the chinks in the logs to reveal a very large, grasping, clawed paw.

The love of adventure had brought me to "Happy Clam Beach," as we named our fresh, salty slice of Alaskan wilderness. A seven-passenger de Havilland Beaver floatplane had separately delivered the two of us lovers to the remote area known for its enormous and plentiful razor clams. My high school boyfriend was also an adventurer, and at the time, in the mid-'70s, I would follow him anywhere. That summer, I'd followed him first to Kodiak, Alaska. After quickly getting fed up with life in a fish cannery, Eric met a group of Alaska Natives who invited him to join them in their own enterprise of digging razor clams to sell to fisherman for crab bait. It was a much more profitable scheme than working in a smelly cannery. As for me, I lasted just two days in the salmon cannery. The only job offered to women was cleaning and scraping fish guts in a claustrophobic assembly line, which pissed me off enough that I boldly helped myself to a beautiful King salmon—which I cooked and ate on the beach in Homer before joining Eric on the wild Kenai Peninsula beach seventy-five miles away.

We settled in remote Kukak Bay, close to Katmai National Monument and the Valley of Ten Thousand Smokes. We created our camp from daily hauls of logs, driftwood, and other flotsam and jetsam from the beach. Eventually we had enough to scrap together a small, one-room, driftwood log "cabin" across the bay from where the handful of other clam diggers stayed. The irregular shapes of the wood we scavenged left considerable space between stacked logs, which we chinked or stuffed with moss and lichen gathered from the upland forest.

For three months we stuck to our simple daily routine, timed by the tides. Wake up, make food, hike two miles to the beach, dig clams, haul clams back to camp, hoist burlap bags of clams up on poles to keep wildlife from poaching them, eat clams, make a campfire, enjoy a "roll in the hay," and then crash hard on the plank beds that lined our cozy hut. I entertained that someday *National Geographic* would publish my submission about this magical place. Each week, timed with a high tide, a floatplane would land in the bay to exchange our clams for supplies and a little money—if we'd had a good week. I was completely and pleasantly immersed in this adventure in the wilds until Fuzzy became an unwanted variable in our routine.

Four-hundred-pound, cinnamon-tinged Fuzzy was one of a dozen beautiful Alaskan brown bears that shared their beach with us, their guests. All the bears except Fuzzy roamed the area while keeping a respectable distance as they fed on razor clams, sedges, and salmon. Fuzzy, on the other hand, visited our camp at daybreak for seven days straight. This bear was bold, "friendly," and powerfully troublesome. With each visit, we became progressively apprehensive about every step we took on that beach. We'd bang cans noisily and with caution as we traversed our well-worn path across the open meadow. Long, sleepless nights grew more torturous, our ears pricked, waiting to hear a twig snap or a rustle in the sand. One dawn we rose to catch sight of one of our backpacks—the one containing our camp stove and other essentials—being hauled off down the beach. We felt stalked, haunted, and hunted by an intelligent and powerful enemy. When would it come? Where would it appear? What should we do?

Eric and I became increasingly irritable, argumentative, and on edge, always anticipating a surprise visit. Fuzzy had already sniffed out

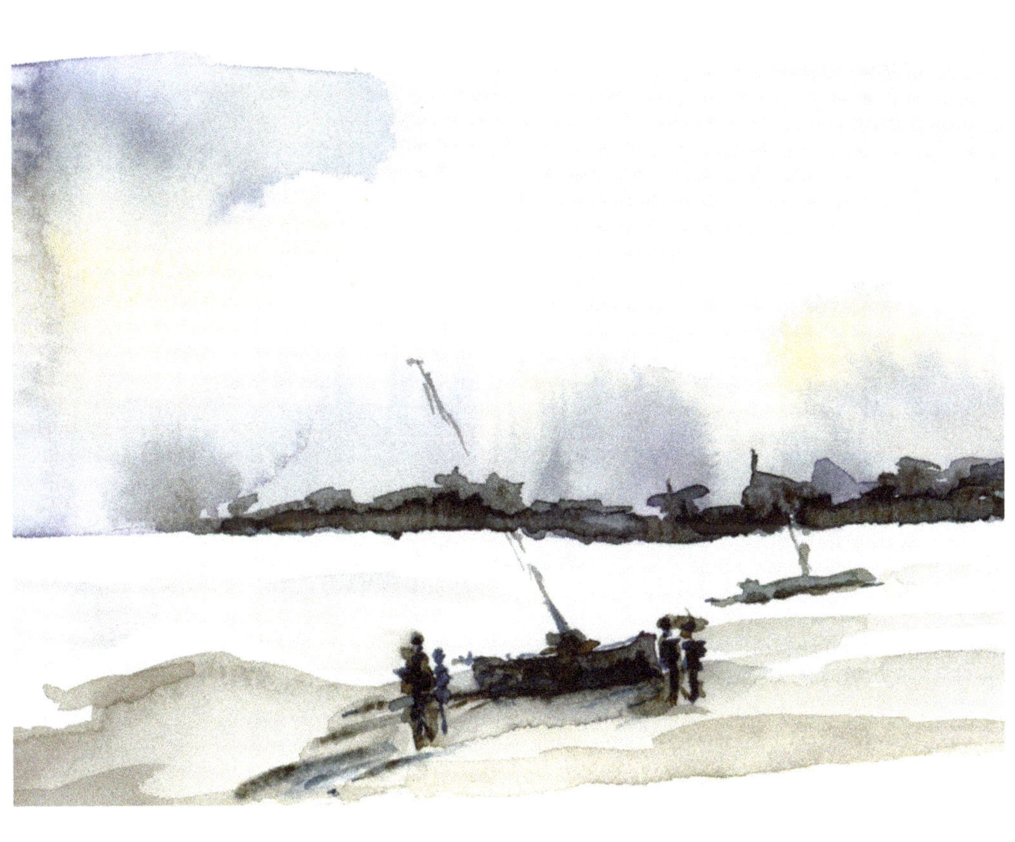

our bountiful and all-too-convenient stash of clams, which we'd enclosed in a makeshift shed and strung high on the poles. These clams were our trading beads, and now they were in constant jeopardy. Fuzzy's routine and aggressive camp visits were destroying our commerce, threatening our peace of mind, and violating our safety.

Now, on ten-foot-tall Fuzzy's eighth daybreak visit, here was the bear reaching through and inside our fortress with a paw the width of our camp skillet and removing a section of roof with a mere flick of one of its five front claws. Imagine sweeping a mosquito from your friend's forehead—only your hand is a four-inch-long razor blade. As I watched in horror from my prone position, I felt certain this was the end. But then, suddenly, fearless adrenalin exploded inside me, erasing any training advice to play dead. Bear spray wouldn't be available for roughly another decade. We both had Winchester rifles, and we used them simultaneously. A crystal-clear, ear-splitting round of life-giving shots rang from inside our now roofless fort and resounded across the bay.

Miraculously, one of us penetrated the exact vulnerable spot—a lung or, most likely, the heart. Bruised from the rifles' kickback and spent from fear, Eric and I watched Fuzzy collapse on the sand only moments before we, too, slumped into a sobbing heap. We were relieved—we'd been flirting too long and too closely with danger—but we also felt a deep appreciation and respect for our kill. It's truly a miracle that Eric and I didn't destroy each other when we both fumbled with our rifles that code-red dawn.

Disposing of Fuzzy's body became an insurmountable task. We tried to hide our shame over killing such a beautiful creature by burying it (her, as we discovered) in the sand. The tide, however, managed to reveal more and more of the hidden carcass each day, and the burial mound was a major hazard to our supply line because the floatplane needed a clear landing stretch. On top of that, the carcass attracted a profusion of opportunistic freeloaders and became the site of an aggressive feeding frenzy. Scavengers such as other bears, bald eagles, wolves, and a lone wolverine dug up and scattered Fuzzy's organs along the beach, including her splayed heart. Eastern winds passed over the body and delivered a raw stench across our camp. Our native friends on the other side of the bay came to assist our final effort. Together, we split the carcass open and with the help of kerosene made a futile attempt to destroy the body by fire—which a high incoming tide eventually doused.

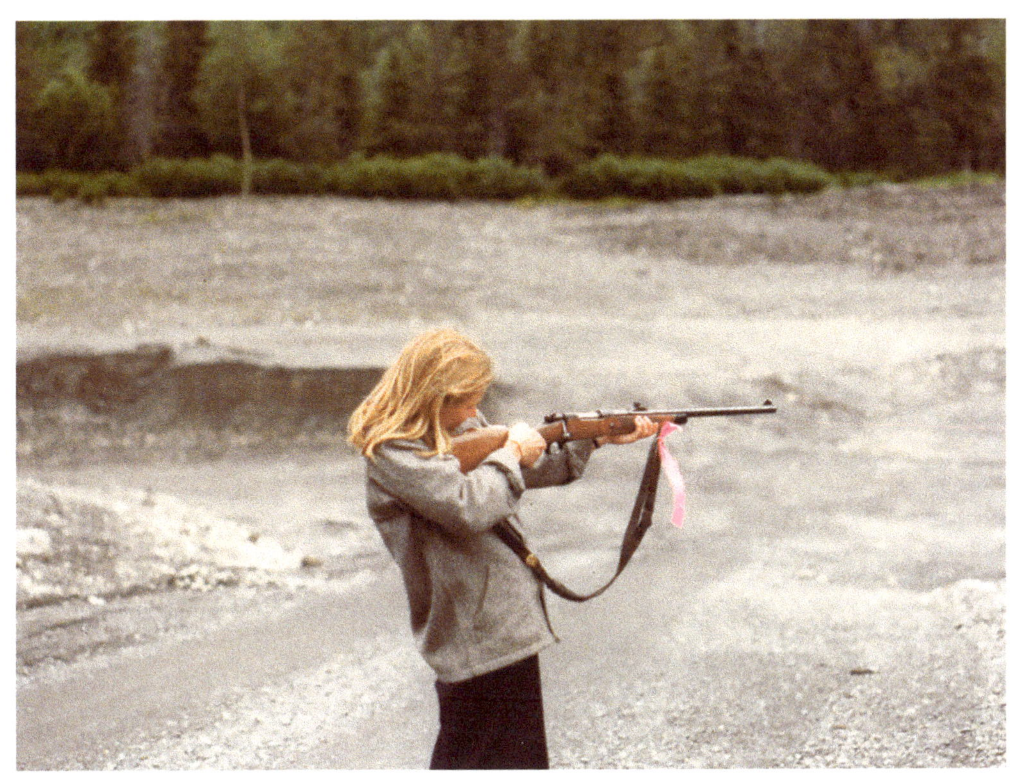

Fuzzy's Beach, AK

Nature was ready to recycle all parts of Fuzzy while we tried to forgive our sensitive souls for disrupting the pattern of life on that wild beach. I did not hate Fuzzy, nor did I resent her. I was consumed by her beauty, power, and intelligence, and filled with remorse. Two lovers on the beach had stopped her young beating heart, cold. I felt regret, guilt, and grief. *Was greed what brought us to Happy Clam Beach?* I asked myself. *Had our folly disrupted the order of nature?* After all, Fuzzy's extended family had been on that beach digging clams for generations.

It was time to leave. The short season was nearly over, and our weather window was closing in. As the floatplane landed in the bay to fetch us, Eric and I stood locked together on that beach, tormented by Fuzzy's heart, which throbbed in our own heavy hearts. As the pilot spun the Beaver around with us now inside, we took a last, long, hard look at that beach, Fuzzy's Beach. Pressing my sniffling nose tight against the window, I scanned the bay from above and caught glimpse of a fuzzy, lone, motherless cub emerging from the far end of the beach.

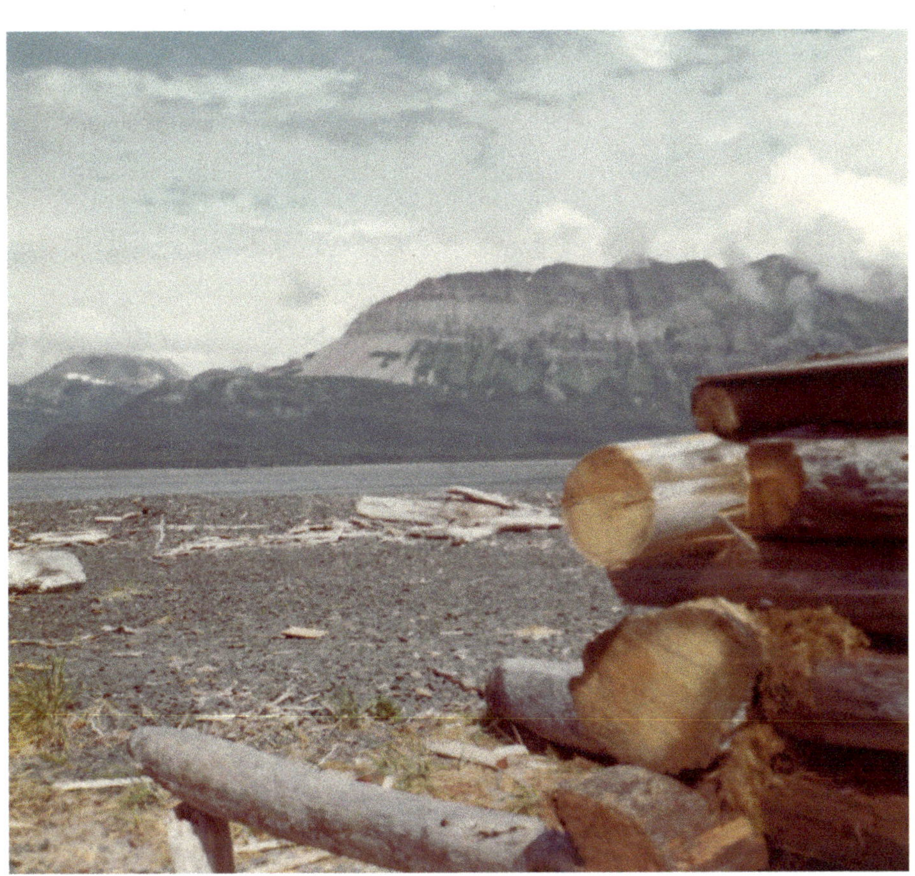

Kukak Bay and the Aleutian Range

Chapter 5

Which Fork?

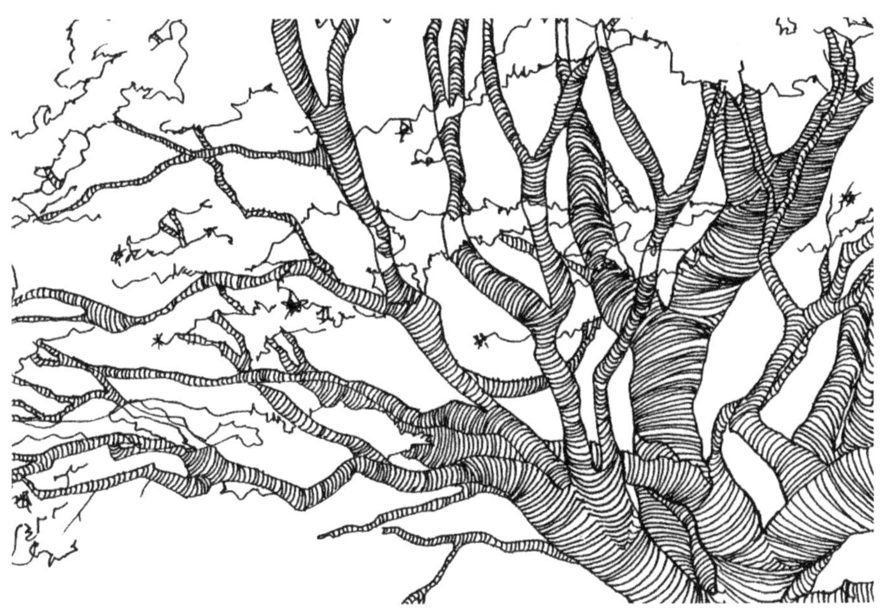

Being cold, wet, alone, starving, and four hundred miles up the Noatak River in the Arctic tundra of Alaska was a desperate predicament, the Noatak River being the longest free-flowing wild river in the United States. But the worst part of this river trip was having lost my boat. It had been thirty-eight days since the Cessna 185 dropped us on a glistening quartz gravel bar high up in the Brooks Range of Alaska. I'd taken a break from college to have a raw and wild experience with the hope of opening a wilderness lodge one day. My Forest Service colleague, Chad, and I set out to paddle to the Arctic Ocean in our collapsible Klepper kayaks with a few supplies, one tent, and an outdated map. Rivers are dynamic and highly changeable with the seasons, so no map would have been accurate anyway. This was the mid-1970s, long before smart phones went public, so the only partially helpful map, a compass, and the elusive sun were the extent of our navigation tools. We were thrilled not to see a single sign of humanity for days, but we also barely saw the sun.

The air was bitingly cold and damp the day we put in on the river, but the sound of the flowing river in the rain was reassuring and constant. While leisurely navigating the current, we observed three grizzlies casually sweeping their paws into the river, snagging unsuspecting salmon. It occurred to me that, if necessary, we could supplement our food rations by catching fish.

By the end of the first wet week, we'd slipped into a rhythm of riding, relaxing, and breathing through the bends in the river, all the while avoiding being sucked into swirling back eddies or colliding with migrating caribou who crossed the river without looking both ways for humans in kayaks. I found myself bouncing over mellow rapids and sliding euphorically down small waterfalls. Every day was both exhilarating and demanding. I lost control and found my boat swept in an unintended direction several times, but the fun was in knowing the river was in charge. The vegetation, although sparse, took on powerful golden hues of fall. A stocky, rarely seen wolverine, about the size of a small bear, accompanied us along the shoreline for a spell as we journeyed further downriver. Each day the river grew louder and louder and the landscape increasingly reflected spring, with budding arctic lupine and tufts of sprouting bear grass. Even when snug in our riverside tent each night, we had to yell to be heard by one another.

Our sports-car-like, highly maneuverable and responsive single kayaks were vehicles on a predictable track to the ocean. The powerful river was our highway and our lifeline. By day fifteen, however, the swollen river had become impetuous, presenting arduous challenges. The color of the river had changed from sparkling clear to frothy and opaque. The snowmelt from the mountains behind us was adding volumes of water. No salmon would ever bite our hooks in such muddled water. Up ahead, the swift river appeared even more confused and turbulent. There were so many forks. Caught in the incessant current while scanning the horizon, I repeatedly wrestled with the question, *Which fork?*

The fiercely braiding river now moved in torrents and had become multiple rivers. Someone had apparently pulled a plug and the whole river was intensely draining out. In several places, we had to carry our kayaks and backtrack through impenetrable landscape to avoid capsizing in impossible rapids and against obstacles. Our attempts to supplement our food stores with fresh fish or game were futile, and by day twenty-one our food rations were mostly depleted. I would stare and drool at Chad's bronzed, muscular forearm while fighting back the desire to chomp on that available red meat. I don't believe he had the same thoughts, but it really freaked me out then—and does to this day—to know how serious I was.

It's hard to say how we got separated. The river was in control. I took one fork and Chad took another. It was day twenty-five. I watched

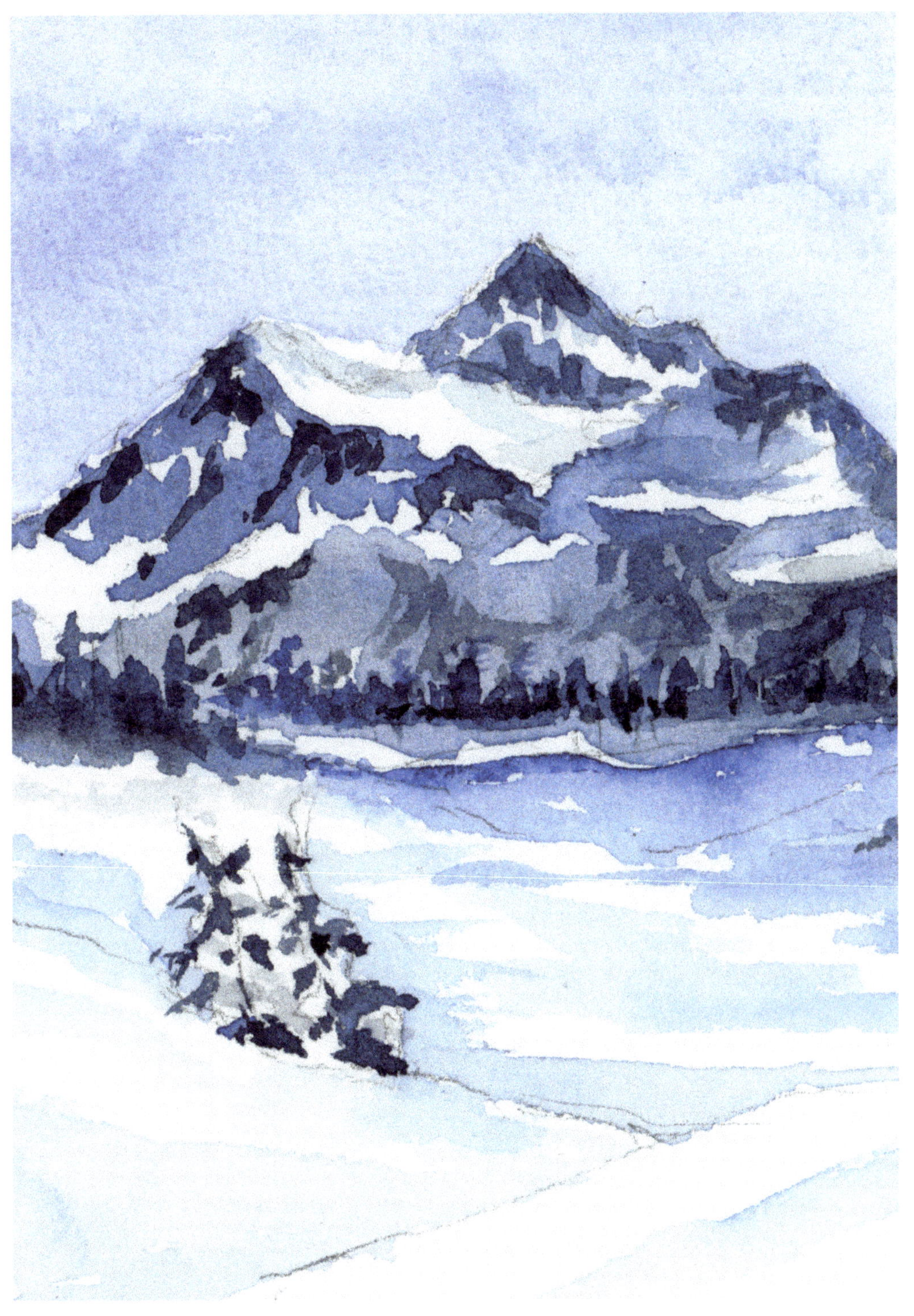

as he disappeared around a bend, but I kept paddling, confident we would reconvene as usual around the next bend, or the next. Hours passed. I kept looking ahead, choosing one fork after another fork. Paddling alone, with only our "pack it out" garbage, a soggy piece of pilot bread, and a can of sardines, I bit my drenched lip hard, listened to my hopeful self, and just continued to flow with the river.

Risky rapids amplified and then washed away repeatedly, over and over. I spent ten fear-embedded days paddling alone and ten blurry solo nights huddled and numb under a makeshift shelter constructed from my paddle and spray skirt. Gathering and eating fiddlehead ferns only slightly boosted my morale. Defying the odds, I scavenged and survived on spawned out salmon from the river's banks and learned from the bears how to eat crowberries, raking them with my own blistered paws.

At daybreak on day thirty-five, ten days after being separated in this vast wilderness, the blinding sun showed up for the first time in more than four weeks. By the braiding and flattening out of the river, I guessed I was about fifty miles from Noatak, a village of a few hundred people. A brilliant arcing rainbow showered a kaleidoscopic display through the spruce and aspen forest. This amazing sight renewed my hope and warded off my impending despair. The flow of the river slowed and the scene ahead started to look like one big sandbar. At dusk, as was my routine, I pulled my kayak up on a bank for the night.

I slept OK that night, but all my hopeful feelings from the previous day vanished when I awakened the next morning. My boat was nowhere to be seen. Gone. Tides come in and tides go out. Apparently, the extreme high tide in the night had floated my kayak away. I tried not to believe that rivers lead to the ocean. The wild river drowned out the sound of my crazy, despondent laugh. *It will do you no good to panic or lose hope*, I coached myself. It worked: I recovered an innate survival instinct and sprang into action, using my paddle as a machete to slap and bushwhack my way downriver through fifty billion mosquitoes and dense groves of willow and Labrador tea. In less than an hour, thanks to our forgiving planet, I miraculously found my skinny blue boat spinning in a distant eddy.

Two hopeful days later, as if a mirage, a camp of four weather-beaten Inupiat villagers, including Chad, appeared as tiny dots in the distance on a sandbar. I'm sure my welcome party had been hoping the river would eventually deliver me, and it did, though weak and about fifteen pounds lighter. In a concert of anticipation, they waved their

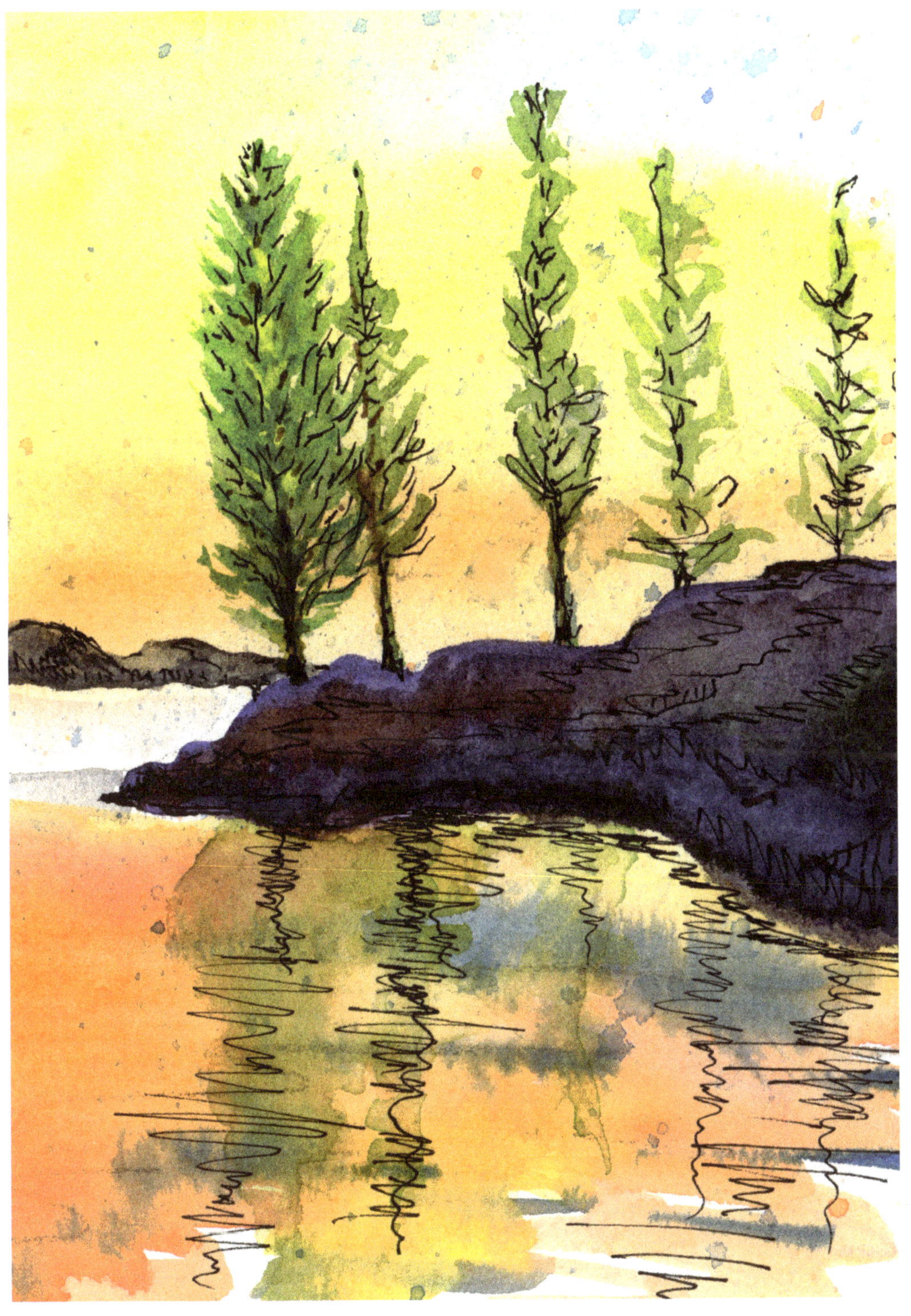

shiny spoons while holding up a tub of akutaq, or Eskimo ice cream. On that sweet, life-affirming day, this unsavory concoction of reindeer fat, seal oil, and freshly ground fish tasted like an incredible slice of some wild heaven.

• • •

My seasonal job with the US Forest Service was ending, and with a long, dark, Alaskan winter looming ahead, I was ready to return to the lower forty-eight and bury myself in a master's degree program in Environmental Science. Chad stayed to continue working with the Forest Service, and we parted ways.

After graduation in 1989, I longed to return to water. This time, it would be salt water. In 1990, a man with the friendliest eyes (who I'd married) and I leased a 500-acre private island in the San Juan Islands of Washington State. Our island was known as Safari Island for the exotic animals that were imported in the 1960's. There, Roy and I created a marine conservation center and program we called Whale Camp. This was not a weight-reducing camp, as some people ridiculously and mistakenly thought when they heard the name, but a program designed to provide guests with total immersion learning adventures in the surrounding marine environment.

The San Juan Islands are home to the southern resident pods of orcas (namely, J, K, and L). For more than a decade, my company, Island Institute, captured the hearts and imaginations of hundreds of kids of all ages. We launched ecotourism, eco-education, and safari-style glamping before those terms were widely used. Back then, you would've found our guests—families, corporate executives, and students—snorkeling in full wetsuits, hiking to learn about native plants, sea kayaking to hidden coves to explore marine invertebrates, cruising to spot whales, sleeping in safari-style tents, and of course, eating Eskimo ice cream in the large log cabin lodge, which I aptly named The Right Fork.

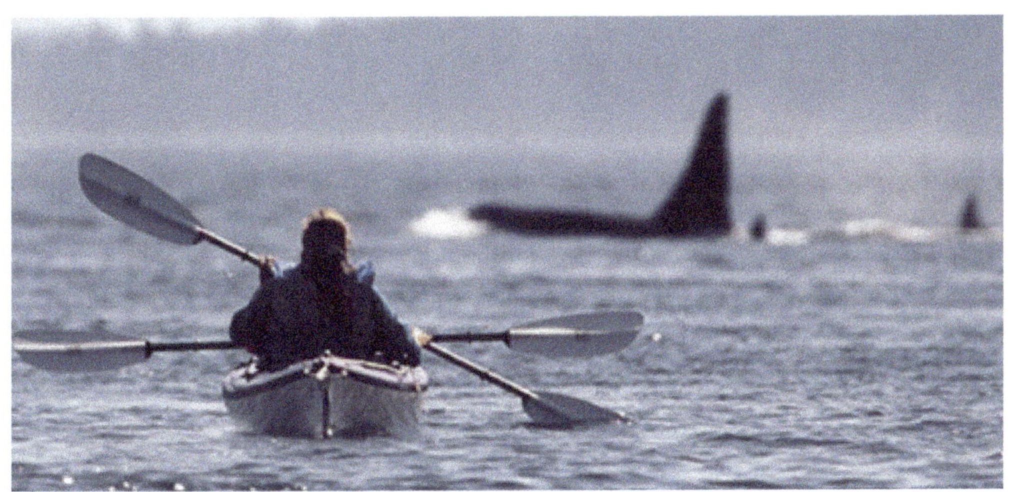

Encounter with orcas

Chapter 6

Uncle Ralph

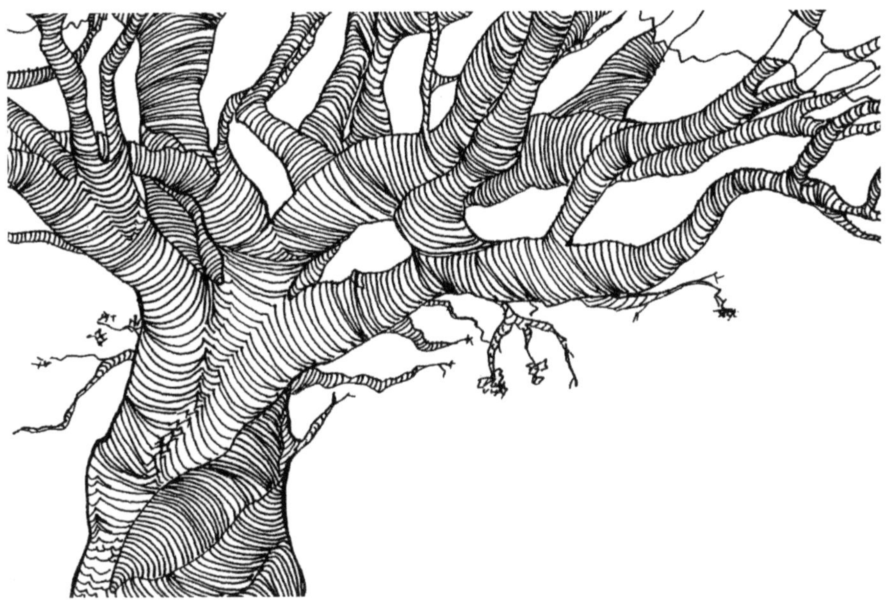

I paddled my canoe as close to the nest as I comfortably could. Alligators are known to run forty miles an hour at a sprint, so I approached with caution even though the nest at Chase Prairie was empty that still morning. Locating and counting alligator nests and their eggs was my first real job out of college and my primary job assignment with the Fish & Wildlife Service at Georgia's Okefenokee Wildlife Refuge. It was impossible to see inside a nest from my canoe. In a time before drones, I had to make careful assessments when approaching a nest and always have an escape plan before landing my canoe and setting foot on a floating bog. Some nests were more than ten feet across, and they could house between thirty-five and ninety eggs.

My daily routine involved mapping routes through the ever-changing water channels of the shallow Suwanee Canal and paddling my assigned canoe out from the ranger station. I petitioned the all-male department to purchase an electric motor for my canoe, but my request met deaf ears. Paddling was tough, but the hardest part of my work was its solitary nature. For an extrovert like me, spending long, lonely days with only the balm of nature for company was challenging. Detached from the world, I soon found myself whistling and conversing with the snapping turtles I spotted along narrow banks, all while sporting the pith helmet my brother had gifted me for graduation. Each day brought me closer to nature; the buzzing and gurgling sounds of the swamp lured me in. Over time I began to proudly imagine myself becoming a solo, seasoned swamp naturalist. And then I met Ralph.

I'd heard talk back at the ranger station about a legendary swamper named Uncle Ralph who lived deep in the endless blackwater. Rumor had it this illusive character knew more about the swamp than all the books in the visitor center's library. And sure enough, on this day along came a bulky old man, disturbing my private lunch break by poling his flatboat over to my canoe at the edge of the canal. In my surprise, I dropped the fried chicken drumstick I'd been enjoying, losing it to a fifteen-foot alligator that had been watching my every move.

As he approached, I eyed the roofing nails Ralph wore in lieu of buttons on his shirt, and then I anxiously turned away. I'd never met a soul while working in the Refuge's 300,000 swampy acres. But while at first I resented and even feared this interruption to the solitude I'd only recently embraced, I was also struck with extreme curiosity and wonder.

I said hello first, but Ralph took it from there, apparently eager for company. This is what I learned: Ralph was from the Seminole Nation and had lived his entire sixty-eight years deep in the Okefenokee Swamp. He knew the area like the back of his hand. He'd watched the prairies burn for almost a year. (Ironically, lightning strikes are necessary for the natural regeneration of these wetlands.) For his entire life, Ralph had been listening to the choruses of frogs and insects, to the screeches of lone bobcats, and to the grunts of thousands of alligators. Ralph personally knew the very alligator that ate my lunch. Ol' Roy, as Ralph called him, had previously snatched a small dog off a leash from the refuge dock and abruptly stopped a tractor mower in its jaw before dragging it deep into the current of the St. Mary's River. Ol' Roy, said Ralph, had already been full of bad habits when the watery refuge was first established.

Ralph had endless stories. He told fascinating tales of the alligators' spring courtship "water dances," and . . . I asked a million questions, he answered, and I listened deeply.

With a toothless smile, Uncle Ralph invited me aboard his flatboat. I couldn't resist and left my canoe in the mangroves. He skillfully placed his hand-carved push pole into the peat-filled wetland, and we glided about ten miles down the Suwanee Canal toward his home on Floyds Island. With Ralph's help, I glimpsed a green heron sneaking quietly through the underbrush of bay and Titi shrubs. Ralph pointed out a sharp-shinned hawk's nest on top of a grand cypress tree, and a sandhill crane shielded by a screen of yellow-eyed grass. His boat slid through the dark, acidic water, creating ripples that overturned water-lilies and sent beads of water sliding down leaves of the abundant never-wet plant.

As we moved deeper into the dreamy swamp environment, the air became increasingly still, heavy, and very warm. Ralph slowed his boat in a small, secretive pool, dipped his metal cup into its cool, brown water, and took a long drink. Legend has it that sea captains used to sail miles out of their way to load up on this tannin-laden, tea-colored "blackwater," which would stay fresh in their barrels for months.

We crossed Chase Prairie, an open, sun-filled waterway, where Ralph noted that the marsh marigolds and carnivorous pitcher plants were being slowly replaced by black gum trees through natural succession. Here, the water trail began to grow darker and narrower. Ralph took care not to brush against the lush underbrush, for we'd already discovered numerous ticks and red bugs on our legs and arms. He worked hard to dodge and push blobs of peat (or "blow-ups") out of our way. As vegetation decays in this swamp, carbon dioxide and methane gas are released, forcing masses of earth to rise and float to the surface of the water. The indigenous Creek or Muscogee people named the swamp Okefenokee, which spoken in Hitchiti language sounds like "okee" (translates to "water") "fanokee" (translates to "shaking"). The word roughly means "bubbling water" or "trembling earth"—that's what the natives felt as they walked over the peat. I couldn't resist jumping up and down on the trembling earth, a floating waterbed-like bog. It appeared to be solid land but was more like an oversaturated sponge, impossible to walk upon for long.

Ralph had generously shown me more than ten new alligator nests by the time we arrived at Floyd's Island in the late afternoon. I was thrilled. It had been a day of new discoveries, both external and internal. This chance encounter had taken me away from work routines to a place of wonder, awe, and deeper understanding.

Floyd's Island was true solid ground, and there was Uncle Ralph's one-room pine log cabin. A young white-tailed doe watched as we tied up his flatboat. The cabin, which some homesteader most likely built before Franklin D. Roosevelt established the Refuge in 1937, had a dirt floor, a steep roof, and a small porch. It appeared that Ralph slept in a loft accessed by a ladder. I spotted rattlesnake skins hanging to dry out by a small garden. No surprise that Ralph appeared to be quite self-sufficient. He wanted to show me an Indigenous ceremonial mound, a place very special to him as he was part Creek. I felt like I was in a fairy tale when I stumbled across a rose-colored arrowhead and several pieces of pre-Columbian Native American pottery. Questions flooded my mind as the sun set, backlighting swamp silhouettes draped in Spanish moss.

As I got to know Ralph that day, I realized that he and I were reflections of each other, much like how the still, black swamp water reflects a mirror image of the gentle, lofty white clouds overhead. We were two solitary souls, both fascinated and lured by the swamp, and both with potential to share and inspire. Had I paddled away when he interrupted my lunchtime solitude, I would've missed out on a legend. Had he hidden from me, he would've missed an opportunity to share the richness of all he knew.

The boat ride back to my canoe in the cool evening breeze was all too swift. The button-nails on Uncle Ralph's shirt jingled softly. Our exchange and connection that day in this magnificently eerie, watery environment of Okefenokee had been much like the swamp itself—teeming with life and mystery.

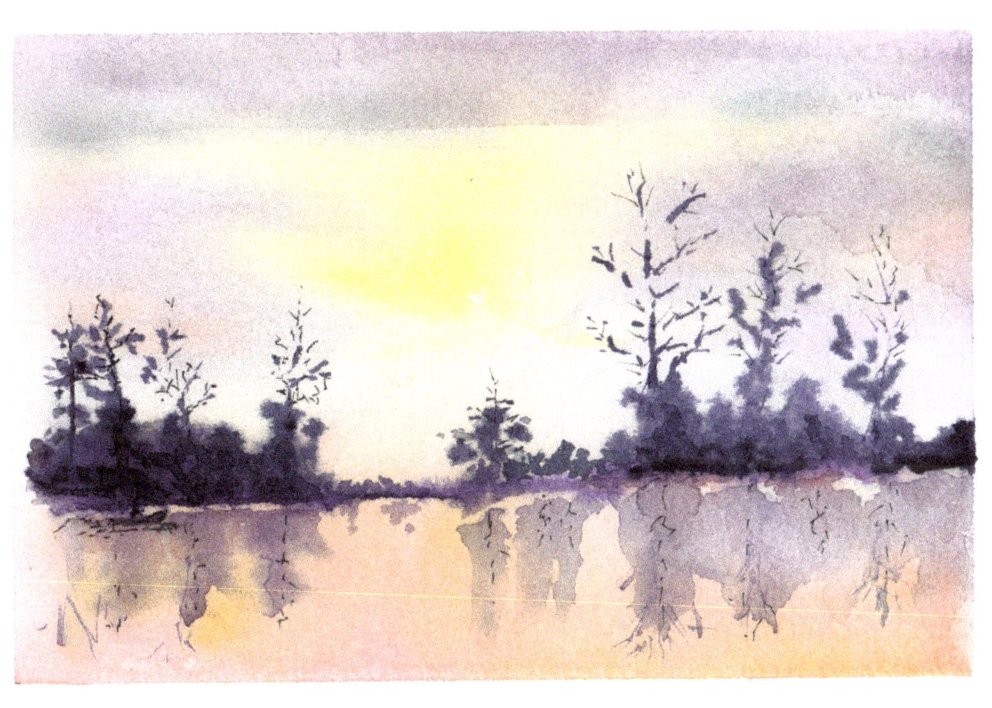

Chapter 7

Just Keep Swimming

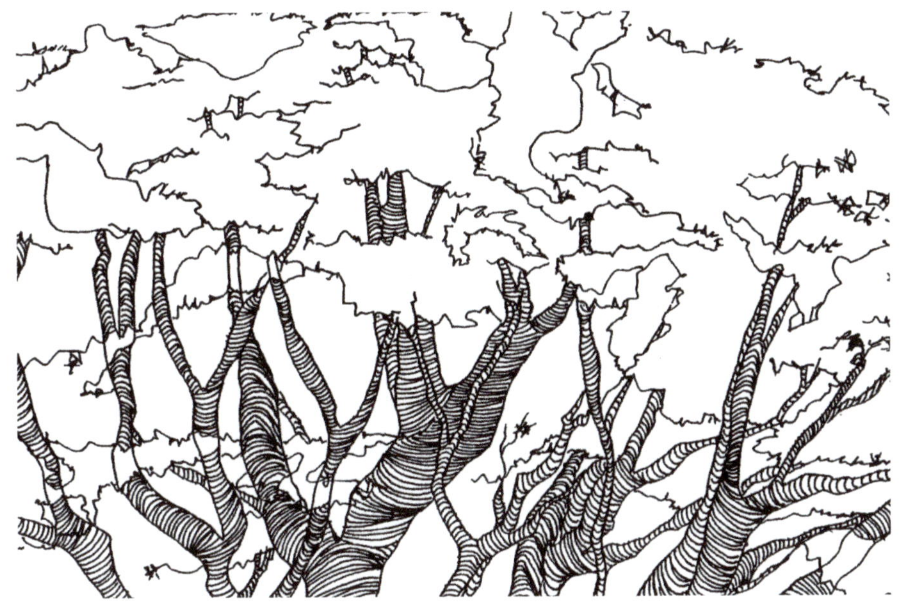

Our Belizean guide Captain Kent looked me straight in the eye and said, "Now's your chance. Jump!"

How did he know that swimming with wild dolphins was a dream hidden away deep in my nature-loving spirit? I'd organized a small group to travel to this atoll, which is part of the Belize Barrier Reef, the second-largest coral reef system in the world, a diverse ecosystem about twenty miles off the coast of Belize City. It was the early 1990s. I was a young mother accompanied by my family—two toddlers who were captivated by the tarantula they'd discovered on one of their pillows in our rustic eco-lodge bungalow, and my adventurous husband—plus our nanny Jane (who we called Jane 2) and dear friend Liz.

I froze like a deer in headlights for a fleeting second but then impulsively jumped, fully clothed, from the inflatable into the watery world of Turneffe Atoll. Captain Kent tossed me a mask and snorkel. I fumbled with fins. The lumpy, sapphire water felt warmer than the air but looked deep and vast. Spontaneously, I held my breath and dove down. *What do I hope to experience?* I wondered.

A wall of bubbles initially blocked my vision, but high-pitched squeaks and squeals resounding from dark depths assured me that dolphins were nearby. As I came up for air, I had the distinct feeling of something brushing past me. Suddenly, two bottlenose dolphins were in my face, circling, twisting, whirling, and alternating between darting a distance away and then sprinting in return. I watched, enraptured, as two twelve-foot-long mammals performed loops around and over me. I found myself waving as they shot by my outstretched hands—silly but trying to make a connection. They repeatedly nosed me without touching. They seemed to be smiling loudly. I know I was smiling between my clenched teeth. This moment was a dream.

Not wanting to miss a second of this mesmerizing encounter, I zoomed to the surface for a gulp of air. Returning below with wide eyes, I counted more than twenty wild dolphins, several with small, pink-skinned babies dancing about beside them. Compelled to communicate and blend in with the dolphins, I mimicked their high-pitched chatter. Naturally, they were in charge. Swimming with them was on their terms. As if I were fifteen again, I silently named the mega-friendly one Oscar. I watched Oscar cock his head from side to side, much like a friend would do while listening compassionately. I was lost in time. At one close pass, Oscar stopped and looked directly and deeply into my eyes.

Almost forgetting to breathe, I was completely present in mind and body, glued to an outrageous, meditative moment. Oscar's oval-shaped, dark-red eyes, surrounded by a pale white ring, moved independently, seemingly looking in two directions at once, keeping one watchful eye on its pod while the other eye intently focused on me. I was surrounded by loud clicking sounds and tried to imagine Oscar's panoramic view and what it might be thinking. Shaded grey streaks on its body resembled a beautiful charcoal drawing. I surfaced again for air and, as if mimicking me, several dolphins also surfaced with loud exhalations. I was deeply moved by our syncopated dance.

The Atlantic bottlenose dolphin has a three-inch beak or snout or rostrum that protrudes from its face. Recalling Captain Kent's story about dolphins using tools to open his lobster pots, I snapped out of my trance, hit with a stroke of anxiety. This thousand-pound, wild carnivore was not the TV series Flipper. It occurred to me that one of them could easily get aggressive and ram me, grind me with its one hundred teeth, or spear me with one poke of its pointy beak. Dolphins are both carnivorous predators and prey—for sharks. Amidst this watery world, I thought about unpredictability and about how no life ever goes as planned. Then, choosing to believe in the best outcome, I tossed the passing wave of anxiety aside.

Heart pounding, I abruptly resurfaced into the light for air, and then quickly felt compelled to go back down. Following diagonal shafts of light below, I descended. Kicking hard, I thought about the power of nature, the wonder of life, and the importance of the ocean. I thought about our vulnerabilities with and our violations of nature. I thought about life's triumphs and tragedies. With the light also comes the dark, and how we navigate those two realities makes us stronger.

Filling my lungs again, I returned below one last time to witness a euphoric but brief, spell-binding grand finale. A spectacular explosion of about one hundred swirling dolphins filled my vision before their shadows promptly disappeared into the darker depths. As the pod's clicking sounds faded in retreat, I dog-paddled back to the dinghy with the entire cetacean extravaganza forever imprinted in my mind's eye.

The day's reward was a simple yet powerfully inspirational message that will stay with me for the rest of my lifetime: Go for it and just keep swimming.

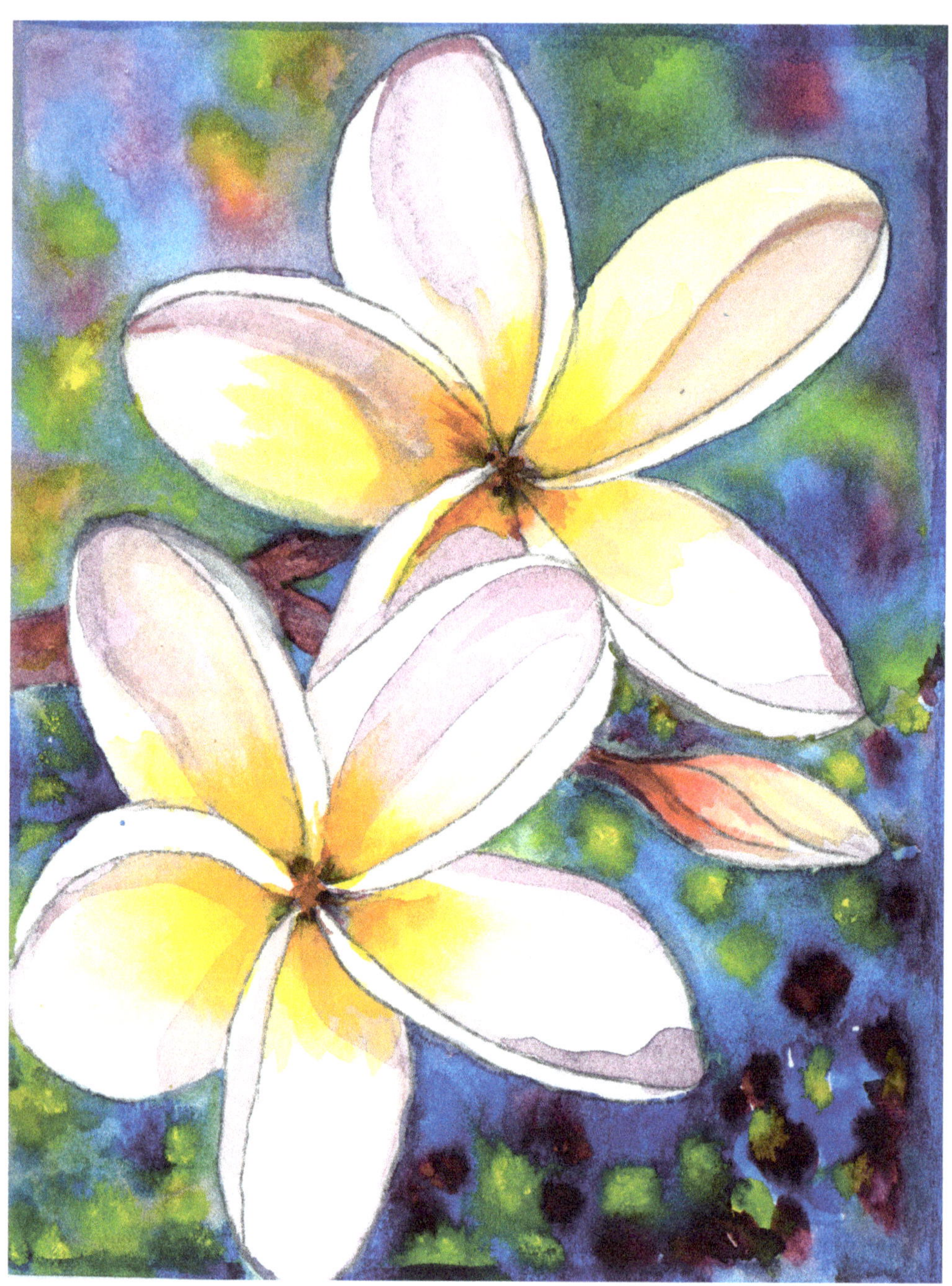

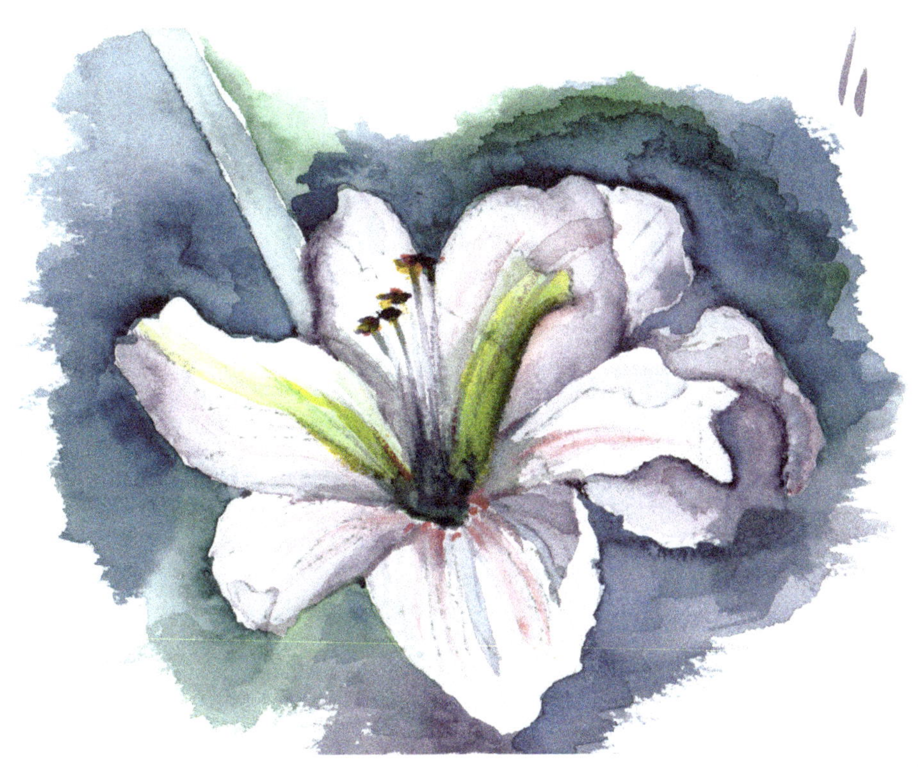

Chapter 8

The Last Interview

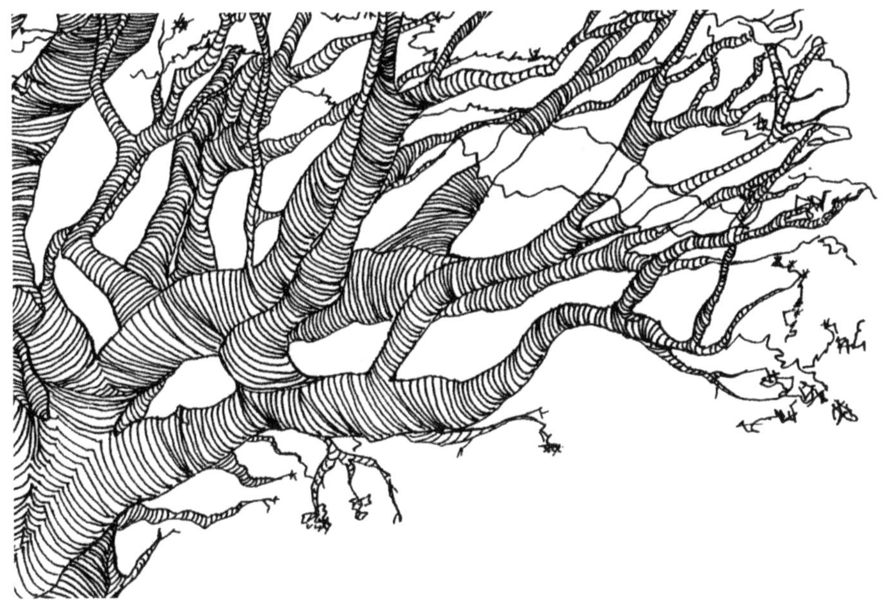

My mind floated like interminable mist as I crossed the wet parking lot, carrying props for my presentation. Starbucks seemed like a good place to kill an hour before heading to the interview, despite my preference for artisanal coffee and hanging out at cuter coffeehouses, which were abundant in Seattle. Watching a constant stream of high-speed cupping connoisseurs ordering to-go cups of designer java helped to distract me and settle my nerves. I shuffled my old-school index cards repeatedly, reviewing my notes and rechecking my phone for the time and exact location for my interview, somewhere in Pioneer Square.

I'd been applying for a variety of conservation education positions at utilities, nonprofits, and consulting firms. Given how the last hiring committee had described my résumé as "sparse," and the fact that I was in my mid-fifties, a mother of two high schoolers, and had been out of a job for over a year, I felt anxious about this interview—about any interview.

"Okay, we are ready for you," one of the members of the hiring committee announced after I'd been waiting in the corporate office's designer entryway for at least half an hour. Then, she muscled her way into the boardroom ahead of me.

I strolled in and was immediately directed to a stiff chair at the head of a ridiculously long conference table.

"We're going to ask you twenty questions, and then it will be your time to deliver your five-minute presentation, which will be timed," said Trudy, one of the five interviewers, from a distance at the far end of the table. "Each time the buzzer goes off, you will be asked the next question until we are through. The entire interview will take no longer than one hour. Time permitting, we will give you a few minutes at the end to ask questions."

Having been laid off from three career-type jobs, I was anxious to reach for what was available in a tight job market. I realized from its description that the job wouldn't exactly be fitting a round peg into a round hole, but "fake it until you make it" was my trusty motto, and applying to this conventional corporate job seemed like a wise move. With a new 'do and a new attitude, I was ready to take on the world.

The tall gal with trendy glasses who'd escorted me into the windowless room, jumped in with the first question. She was thirty-something with a few facial tattoos and piercings in both her nose and ears. Her thick pink hair flashed like a strobe light from across the expansive table as she flipped it over and over between her fingers.

"My name is Sunshine. I will ask you the first question, and then my colleagues and I will take turns. How does that sound?" With barely a pause, she continued. "How do you juggle multiple projects at once and give us some examples of how you deal with pressure."

I was already feeling the pressure. While contemplating Sunshine's question, I got lost in a vivid flashback from 1978: I'm twenty five and traveling with an improvisational theater troupe out of Helena, Montana, where juggling balls and boyfriends is not only a lifestyle but a paying job. Our colorful and talented troupe travels throughout the western states, to native communities, and to Canada, teaching audiences about energy conservation through drama and theater. A gymnasium floor full of squirming elementary schoolchildren waits for our opening act. The announcer cries out, "The New Western Energy Show now presents you with an ancient proverb, 'The Frog Does Not Drink up the Pond in Which it Lives.'" An adult-prompted applause erupts from the packed house as I emerge from behind the drapery dressed as a raven, juggling balls around the protruding beak of the black leather mask I took weeks to craft.

"I have extensive experience in handling multiple projects and partner interests," I improvised in reply to Sunshine's question. "For example, in my last job, I juggled many balls and took the lead on responding to diverse customer requests."

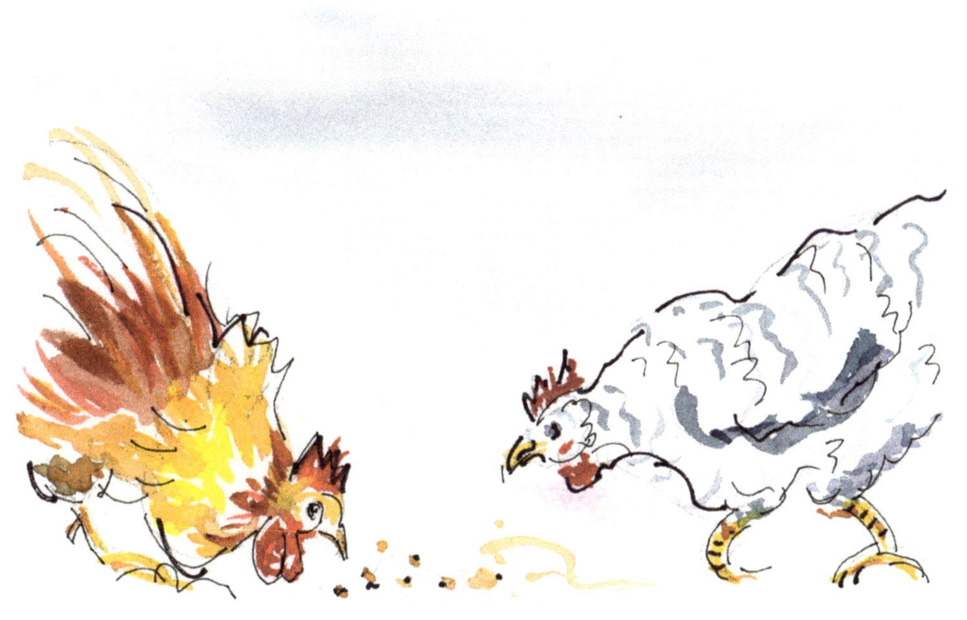

The five committee members glanced away from me in unison to scribble notes on their individual scorecards.

"Tell us more about how you handled a particularly high-pressure or challenging situation," Dave, another person on the hiring committee who I'm guessing was a bully back in high school, boldly interjected. With his too-tight shirt exposing large, bulging muscles, he must've spent all his spare time at the gym. Big Dave took a loud slurp from his coffee and waited for my reply.

My mind flashed on the frustration I'd felt in trying to silence a neighbor's racket-making rooster while I was on an important call. That was certainly a high-pressure situation. I'd been nervously preparing for and awaiting a prearranged phone/computer interview. At the exact time my phone rang, from out of nowhere a loud rooster cruised through the open door of my Hawaiian vacation cottage. The squawking rooster sounded like a high-pitched scream or—more precisely—like an air raid siren. To complete the mess, I disappeared from the interview screen when my wheeled office chair collapsed, sending me to the floor with a whack.

I'm not sure exactly how I responded to Big Dave, but for a split second I really wanted to tear off my interview mask and reveal my authentic self to this serious-sounding, ladder-climbing team. I wanted to share a most challenging experience that had involved guiding youth in the wilds of Southeast Alaska. I'd set out from the Outdoor Education Camp in Juneau to find Lost Lake with ten sixth graders, a "Ten Essentials" survival kit, and a compass. It was supposed to be one night out, practicing survival and compass skills, but we got lost trying to locate Lost Lake.

We were more disoriented than lost, but by the third day's nightfall, the panicked group began to break down, something akin to *Lord of the Flies*. Some kids tried forcibly to lead, many just sat whining, and some wandered off in their own non-direction, bushwhacking while moaning through clouds of mosquitoes and dense spiny devil's club. A few smart kids and I found a stream, and then a small waterfall, and followed it downhill to Eagle River. Back at base camp, however, it had been called in by radio as an "official disaster." I was in charge of this wilderness challenge until the Coast Guard helicopter rescue team arrived upriver in four twenty-five-foot-long inflatable rafts. In the end, no one was irretrievably lost or hurt.

I was lost in my thoughts, thoughts that didn't seem to fit around this boardroom table or with this interview team. I began to formulate a clever response for Big Dave but didn't get the chance to deliver it. To my relief, the buzzer signaled the next question, sparing me from having to reply and attempt to bridge a widening gap.

Britt, a skinny-lipped, lanky blond, looked up from his laptop to query me. "What podcasts do you listen to, Jane?" He kept stroking his hair backward on his head, annoyingly.

This question completely threw me off guard, and my mind attached itself not to "podcast" but to the word "pod." I once owned a commercial boat, the M/V Navigator, one of the first vessels to offer whale watching excursions in the San Juan Islands while assisting in marine research, including how marine traffic affects the vocalizations of resident J, K, and L pods of orca whales in Puget Sound, Washington. I doubted that preppy Britt had ever seen an orca, or knew anything about the scandalous hunt and capture of seven orcas from the super pod of ninety whales trapped in Penn Cove, Whidbey Island in 1970. Five died in the netting process, including a female attempting to reach her tiny calf. I bet he didn't know that either.

"I don't listen to podcasts," I said. I neglected to reveal that I didn't know what a podcast was.

By the last exhausting question, I wondered what time it was and whether we were closing in on the moment of my presentation. I'd begun to view Sunshine, Trudy, Dave, and Britt as robots, what with their automatic, well-rehearsed, unconscious, mechanical ways of speaking and moving.

"Would you please repeat the question?" I asked Britt while glancing down the expansive table, noting how bored Bob looked. I thought perhaps he should be retired. I lamely answered another well-greased question with my own practiced jargon, using words such as "collaboration," "organic growth," "vision," and "innovation."

These people are so cut and dried.

Whatever happened to conversation?

Are they afraid of real discussion?

I had the strong feeling that this foursome was more interested in what they would be ordering for lunch than in interviewing me. During a pause, I began to contemplate using my last $100 to start my own business focused on environmental education.

They bowed their heads, their attention lost to filling out my evaluation. Then bored Bob announced the final question: "How do you deal with a crisis?"

I'd been feeling like I should bail out the boardroom door, but this question woke me up. My mind raced. I recalled how my roommate in college had thought she could fly after consuming some party punch laced with chemicals, and how I'd saved her life by stopping her from jumping out our dorm window. I flashed on how cool and calm I'd remained when a cruise ship, Empress of the North, that was traveling north in the Inside Passage struck a submerged rock called Rocky Island in Icy Straits, Alaska. I was working on a different cruise ship in the same area, and as a first responder I organized the rescue efforts of 248 passengers from the rapidly sinking Empress in the middle of a dark, wet night in 2008. Could these office drones even comprehend what it had been like to calm a tourist after her dog, Fluffy, was snatched off the dock by an alligator during my ranger days in the Okefenokee Swamp?

"I have taken the lead in the position of handling multiple crises," I said. For some unknown reason, I slid into the plural of crisis, exaggerating the "es" while ejecting a little spit. "The secret is to keep calm, ask questions, and take charge."

At this point, the final buzzer sounded, marking the end of the interview with no time for my perky presentation.

Giving everyone an inappropriate hug, which spontaneously erupted from my inner child of ageless wonder, I bounded out the boardroom door. I was tremendously relieved and ultra-excited to be on a new personal journey going forward, *not* as a corporate drone. I did not want that job. The realization came as a sudden epiphany. I needed to live a creative life, to create a profession of my own design and purpose, where I was in charge of me. Inspired and invited by no one but myself, I felt suddenly free to be my very own boss in a creative field of my choice.

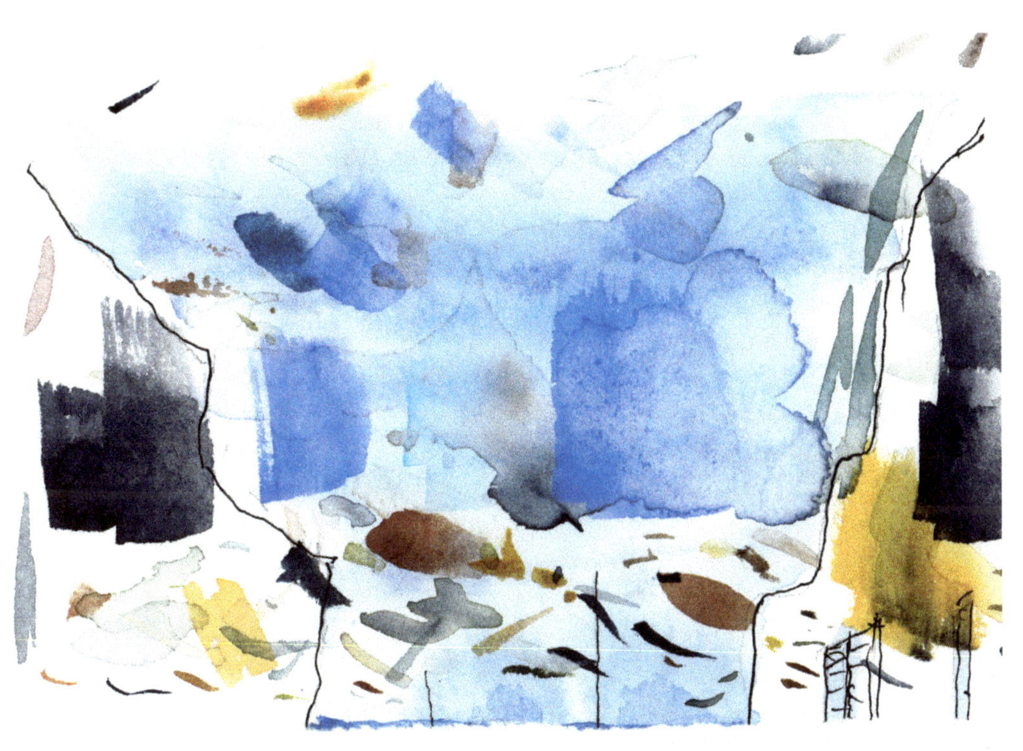

Chapter 9

Lava Refugee

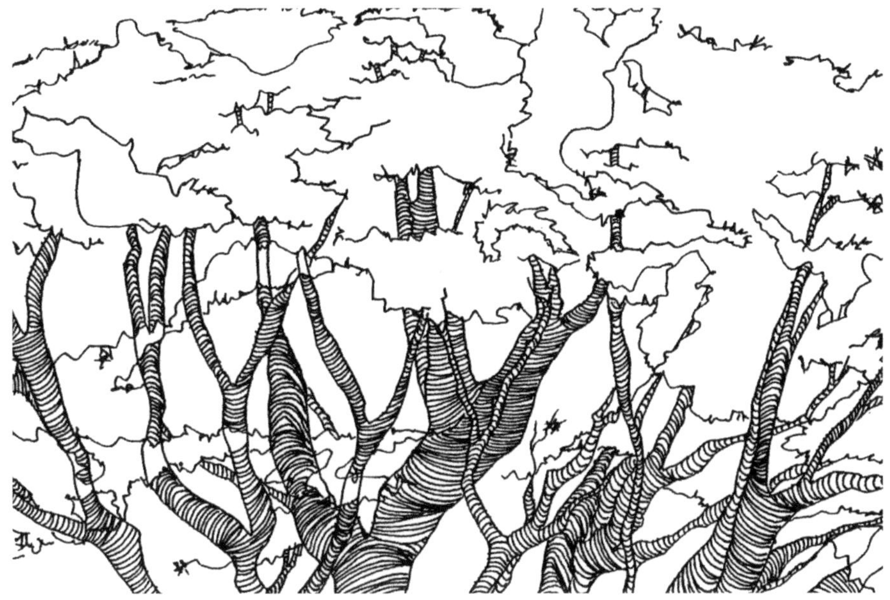

The day Fissure 8 began shooting lava two hundred feet into the air, in May of 2018, runs through my mind's eye like a repeating clip in a scary movie. I'd traveled to the mainland for my son's college graduation, but my neighbor Ella told me over the phone that she was experiencing hundreds of earthquakes a day in my neighborhood on the Big Island of Hawai'i. I was intent on getting home. My succulent white pineapples would be ripe, and my limes would be ready for picking. I knew I lived on an active volcano, but I'd always believed I would be granted a nanosecond in geologic time there—like twenty or maybe thirty years—to delight in Hawai'i's superabundant tropical paradise. The volcano was saying otherwise. Geologic time has its own unstoppable clock.

I'd moved to Hawai'i to work for the state, to teach, and to launch my ecotour company. But now, according to drone reports, the lava lake had overflowed the caldera and was sending tributaries of molten rock toward my home. Despite the risk, I jetted home, and Ella and I were intent on going in. I felt like a wild adventurer journeying to the front line of a threatening target zone. At first nothing looked changed, but as we drove further into the neighborhood, we encountered two fully suited and armed National Guard soldiers in the middle of the road. They signaled us to stop and then warned us that the area ahead was extremely volatile—and closed. We should turn around and leave immediately, they urged. Ignoring their directives, Ella stepped on the gas, and we shot through the barricade.

"You're on your own!" the Guards yelled after us.

Did I have thoughts of doubt and fear as lava was swallowing homes all around? No. I was blindly driven by a mission to get to my home. Traveling beyond the barriers was like entering a war zone. Visibility was analogous to a mountaintop whiteout. The truck crawled through the ash and steam, passing abandoned and stuck cars. I got out several times to investigate crevasses in the road, and layers of fine, glass-like shards of "Pele's hair" lava crunched underfoot. I was hyperventilating inside the stifling respirator I wore, my contacts felt like they were melting on my eyeballs underneath the gas mask, and my heart was racing. Bits of smoking lava stuck in my hair. Lava bombs exploded with the ear-shattering blast of jet engines. It was deafening, extremely dangerous, and not a smart place to be. And yet we persisted.

My cell phone rang. It was my son calling from the mainland. He'd been following civil defense reports and determining by GPS which roads were already impassible and to be avoided at all costs. The call was super short, his last words being, "Mom, get the heck out of there! And don't go back!" But despite knowing that everything in life is "on loan," that nothing is permanent—you can't take it with you, as they say—I felt an urgency to get home to get stuff.

We drove down and backed out of numerous streets to avoid the widening channel of rapidly flowing lava, which crossed the pavement at forty miles an hour in some places, like an open artery pumping lifeblood to the edge of habitable land. Lava rocks pelted the truck. The forest all around was aflame, and eerie blue methane gas seeped out of widening cracks in the pavement. We passed scenes that reminded me of Yellowstone National Park's geysers with their yellow sulfur banks steaming, burping, and crusting over. My familiar Sunday bike route looked like a pulsating red open wound in a charred arm. It was all so mesmerizing, and I felt close to being sucked in. I feared we'd get trapped, that we wouldn't get out. But we pressed onward.

Ella and I had agreed that we'd both get five minutes to retrieve what we could from our homes. In less than a minute inside hers, Ella stumbled out clutching a wooden box, her late husband's ashes. "Let's go!" she barked.

Across the street, the custom wood gate to my property was burning. Nearby lava piles crept like those black snake fireworks that emit

smoke and spew out ash. The sky was a deep, hot sepia color. Everything once alive was dead and defoliated. Dry brown leaves littered the landscape like confetti. All the water had been sucked out of my koi pond, vaporized in an instant along with the vanishing fish.
Creeping up my driveway through this apocalyptic scene, I had a moment of clarity. My mental list of what to grab vanished. Forget the kitchen. Forget the clothes. Of course, forget the furniture and the car. My passport? My grandmother's silverware? No! Forget the stuff! All that was important was my breath going in and out of my respirator.

• • •

She called me a refugee. That was a first. The label felt debilitating. Leila approached to give me a long hug. Then, she took my hands in hers and prayed for me in Hawaiian. This tiny, sweet loan officer had made it possible for me to fund my "forever dream home" on the Big Island six years earlier, and now that I was homeless, she'd just erased my loan with a single click. I didn't ask how or why she did it. I understood that Hawai'i is like that—raw, unpredictable, amazing.

I was now officially a "lava refugee." All my adrenaline had been spent. I felt deflated, like a sad balloon. I sat there in that plush, blue bank chair feeling completely numb. Resilience, I reminded myself.

Leila asked me if I wanted a one-way ticket to the mainland. I stumbled outside.

Seven years later, I can attest that every day is both a risk and a joy. For me, being there in that moment—truly in the wonder of the flow—was frightening and humbling. And yet, it felt natural. New land was being formed, and I was there to witness the Earth's powerful processes. Now that forty feet of hardened lava covers my home, my car, and my neighborhood, people still ask, "What did you grab?" I tell them I grabbed my sensibilities. And now I know the old aphorism to be true: Wherever I am, I am already home.

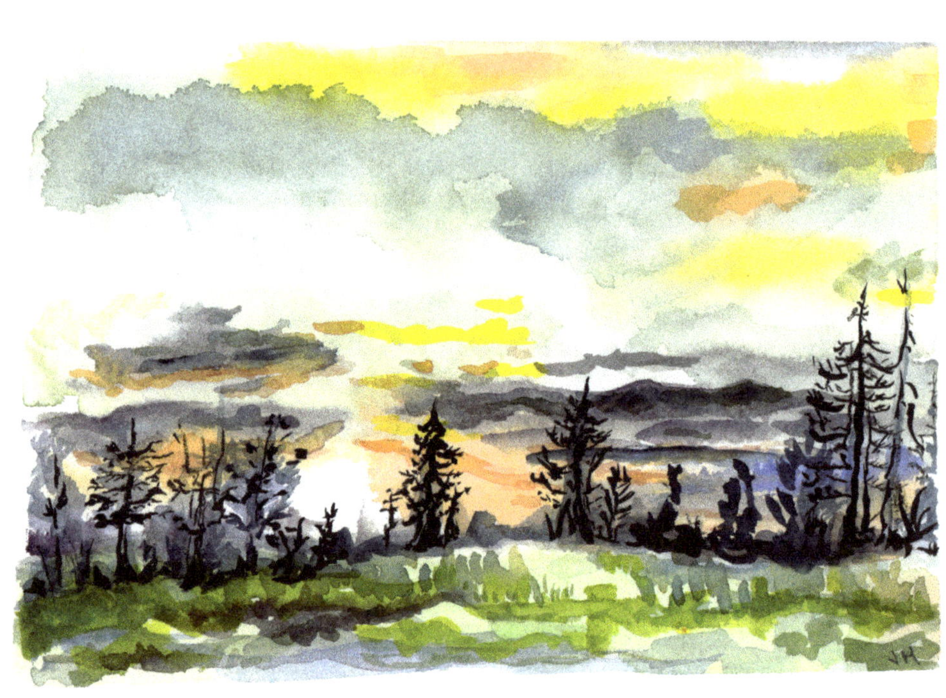

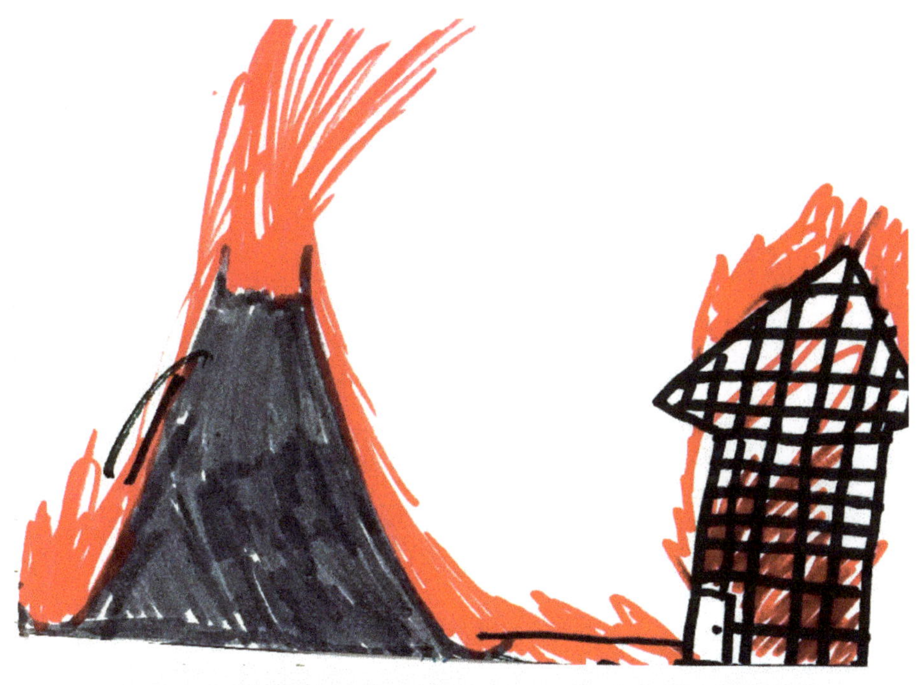

DOUG and JANE,

I KNOW WHAT YOU'RE GOING THROUGH. I'VE LOST MY MOM - JAIL ☹

ALSO, MY GRANDMA'S HOUSE HAD A BIG FIRE. IT WAS SCARY!!!!

WE MOVED TO A HOTEL FOR MONTHS, BUT GOT TO GO HOME RECENTLY. I HOPE YOU CAN TOO!

JAYLAH

Created by a student following the eruption of Kilauea in 2018; used by permission of the teacher

Chapter 10

Zoom Zombies

TEACHING DURING A PANDEMIC, 2020

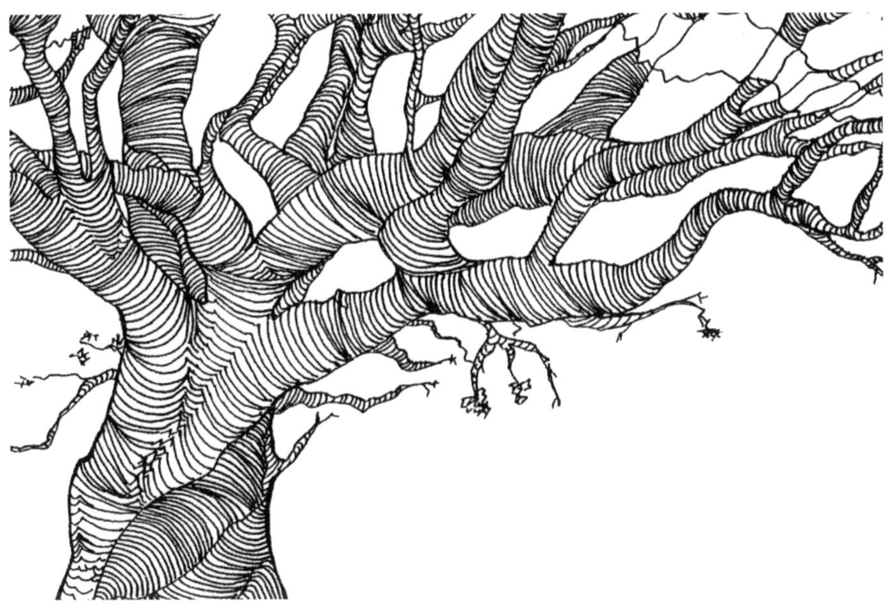

Monday

My cell phone dings at 5 a.m. on a drizzly, grey Monday morning in Seattle. It's an app telling me I have an assignment to teach ELL (English language learners). I jump to get coffee into my system and throw on some clothes. I log into my computer, check the school address, and input the address into my phone for navigation. Whoops, school is closed. Good thing I catch an email stating that the job is remote and won't start for two hours. Going back to bed isn't an option after the coffee, so I pull out my watercolors to pass the time. At the designated hour, I check myself in the mirror. Hair combed? Shirt buttoned? It'll be third graders first, then sixth, then fifth, then fourth. Got it.

I start the Zoom session and greet each third grade ELL student by name as they enter the virtual classroom with a "ding" notification signaling their arrival. I suspect the schedule is wrong, as these faces clearly aren't third graders. Actually, these fifth graders could pass for middle schoolers. I ask for correct pronunciations of their names, as I'm certain I'll butcher them. Some voices are hard to understand, others are too soft, and most won't stop talking. I mute everyone, limiting the chat to only the host (me).

I begin. "Good morning. I am Ms. Jane, your guest teacher for today. What do you like to do on a sunny day?"

I ask each student to respond individually and then pause. All their cameras shut off at once. I wonder whether their regular teacher has gone over Zoom protocols with them. I struggle with student engagement. Since they're learning English and how to write sentences, I wonder whether they understand the question. I decide to ask what their first language is. I'm not sure you're allowed to ask such a personal question, but I proceed to attempt to engage this group of fifth graders from Vietnam, Afghanistan, Africa (I think she said Eritrea), Argentina (Wichí indigenous tribe), Iraq, Peru, and several other countries unfamiliar to me. More than 134 languages are spoken in this school district north of Seattle. I wonder whether I can locate a language translator on Zoom. Many of the students' cameras are still turned off, and mics are now muted, but I hear a chopping sound.

"What are you chopping, Siam?" I ask.

He says he's preparing dinner because he hasn't eaten for days, and his mother is still in Afghanistan.

Their assignment today is to log in and click the green robot on their screen, which will take them to an online learning platform to work on their goals for twenty minutes. Meanwhile, I turn off my mic to mute a siren outside my window. Then, I turn off my camera and pull out my watercolor. After the planned pause, I interrupt and ask the students individually to share their screens so I can see what they're doing. Siam is still chopping. I ask him to show me what he's preparing for dinner and explain that we're looking to find new English language words today. He holds up a green bean and asks me what it's called. He holds up a garlic clove and asks me what it's called. He tells me he wants to go back to in-person school. He wants to make friends. He says he doesn't want to log into the online learning portal because it's designed for babies.

With some scratchy background noise and without warning, Lola disappears from the meeting and doesn't return. August's screen is frozen. I continue to converse with the remaining four students, learning when their birthdays are, what their favorite flavors of cake and ice cream are, and how many brothers and sisters or pets they have. With only minutes remaining, I ask everyone to join a breakout room to have a one-on-one conference with me.

"Tell me one thing you've learned from our time today," I say. I tell them I'll be recording their answers.

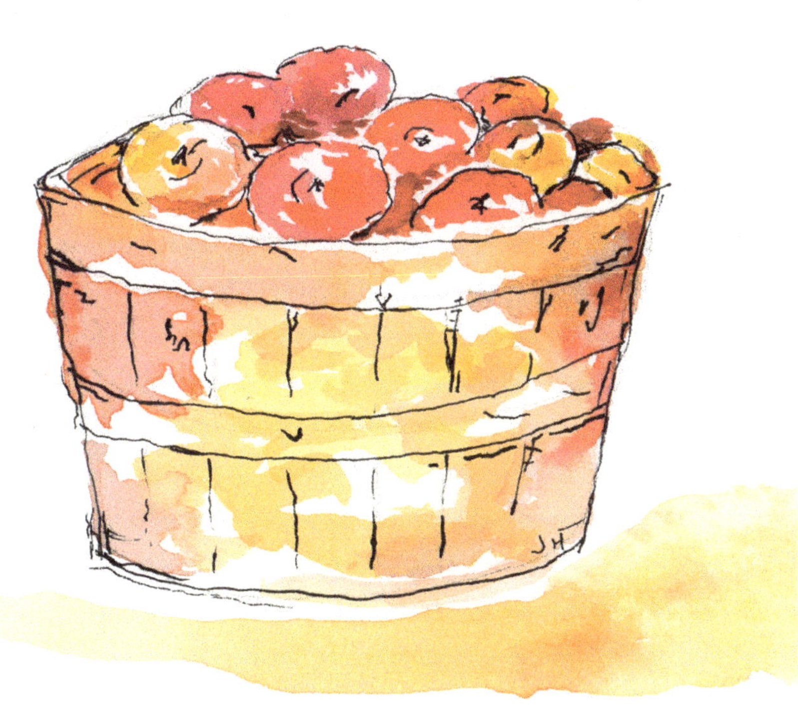
JH

The first student reports that she learned a new word, "mess." Faking composure, I ask her what the definition of the word "mess" is, or to give me an example. She says that learning by Zoom is a mess.

Before disappearing, Lola adds that she has another new word: "zilch." Zilch is what she's learning via Zoom.

Holding up a green bean, Siam asks me what it's called again, and I record him proudly attempting to repeat the two words "green" and "bean." He asks to leave early because he needs to get to the food bank before it closes at three.

Even though I couldn't see most of the faces on Zoom because the students' cameras were either focused on a ceiling fan or had a screenshot of an emoticon instead of their face, I feel overwhelmed with a strong urge to give each student a huge hug. I end the session by clicking "end session" and they're gone.

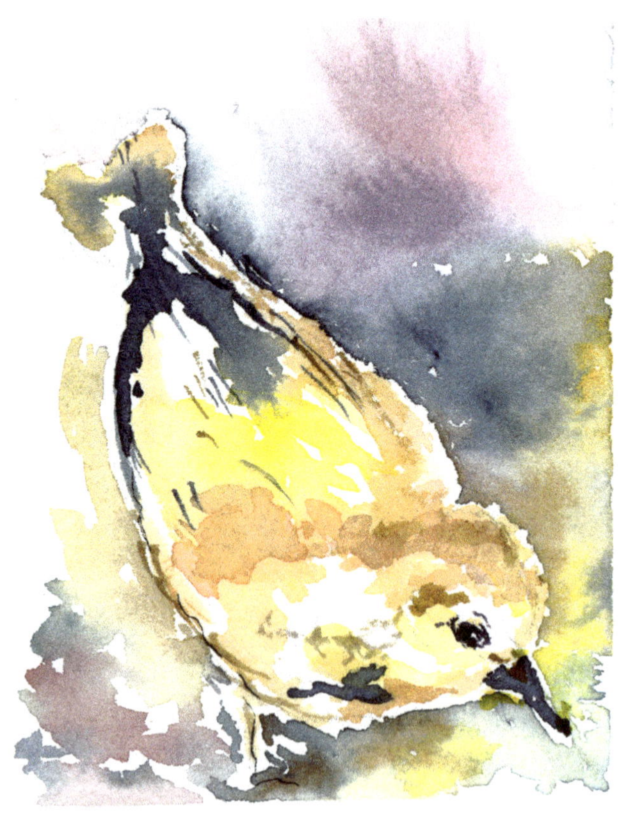

Tuesday

Early Tuesday morning, my phone sounds with an alert that shakes me like a tsunami drill. I accept a guest position to teach English at a high school. I call the school to ask whether this position is to be in person or remote. It's a hybrid class.

Thirty minutes later, I go through the attestation check point outside the school and register at the main office. There, I receive a guest teacher folder and am escorted to a locked classroom. Leafing through the folder, I find a key card and swipe the door open. *How do I turn the lights on?* Moments later, the lights on a timer come on automatically. The classroom appears naked, with nothing on the walls and a very high ceiling with exposed ventilation pipes emitting waves of cold air to keep the school virus-free. At the front of the room is a box of Kleenex and a keyboard with lots of Post-it notes pointing to what needs to be turned on. Logging on with my official credentials, I locate an invitation to a Zoom meeting for the day.

About six students with hoodies drawn and black face masks on slide into the classroom. These few students are attending classes in person. The rest of the class is at home on Zoom. The in-person students aren't the lively kids I remember from a year ago. It's 7 a.m. and no one is talking. I greet the last three in-person students to arrive at the door and receive a few mumbles and grunts in return. They sit socially distanced, far apart from each other in the cold, cavernous classroom.

As instructed in my guest teacher notes, I start the Zoom session on time. To my surprise, their regular teacher appears on the Zoom screen and begins talking to the in-person learners. *Wait, aren't I the teacher for the day?* Then, the teacher speaks to a group of the remote students joining from home. I make several futile attempts to engage the physically present students in discussion, hoping to coax a smile or a question. For most of the past year, students have been learning remotely, starting their day at 9 a.m. With this new 7 a.m. start, in-person students must now get up at 5 a.m. to catch a bus to get them to class on time. They clearly aren't awake. I empathize.

Their teacher finishes speaking. I wonder about the steering wheel visible on his Zoom screen. He's Zooming from his car. I joke that I really like his office, but he replies curtly. It's where he can access the best internet connection, and anyway, at home his crying baby would interfere. Cutting me off, he addresses both the remote and in-person learners, directing them to do silent reading for twenty minutes. I move my camera and turn my body around so I can be seen by the remote learners as well as the six students in the classroom. I wave my hands up and down, struggling to get anyone to crack a smile or react.

This is all so confusing. I'm the in-person guest teacher, in the flesh, and also visible on Zoom to the remote students. At the same time, the regular teacher is Zoom-teaching all the students from his car. *Remain open,* I tell myself. *There's something bigger than you know going on here.*

Later, the office manager explains to me that the students in the classroom today only come to school two days a week. A different set of students attends in person on two other days. When students were asked whether they wanted to return to in-person learning, 60 percent of them voted to return to the classroom, the office manager says. After returning to in-person learning, however, most students changed their minds. Their school wasn't what they remembered. Their fellow students weren't how they remembered. There were no after-school programs, no library, no PE, no shop, and the enforced mask-wearing and dreaded mandatory social distancing were no fun and not at all social.

Today, my attempt to stimulate student discussions, to find a teachable moment, to engage students in conversation or to guide students in learning, fell short. After a year of Zooming from home, student-teacher and student-student relationships will require rebuilding. The greatest good I did today was to click "start Zoom" and offer a bathroom pass to an in-person student with a bloody nose leaking through his mask.

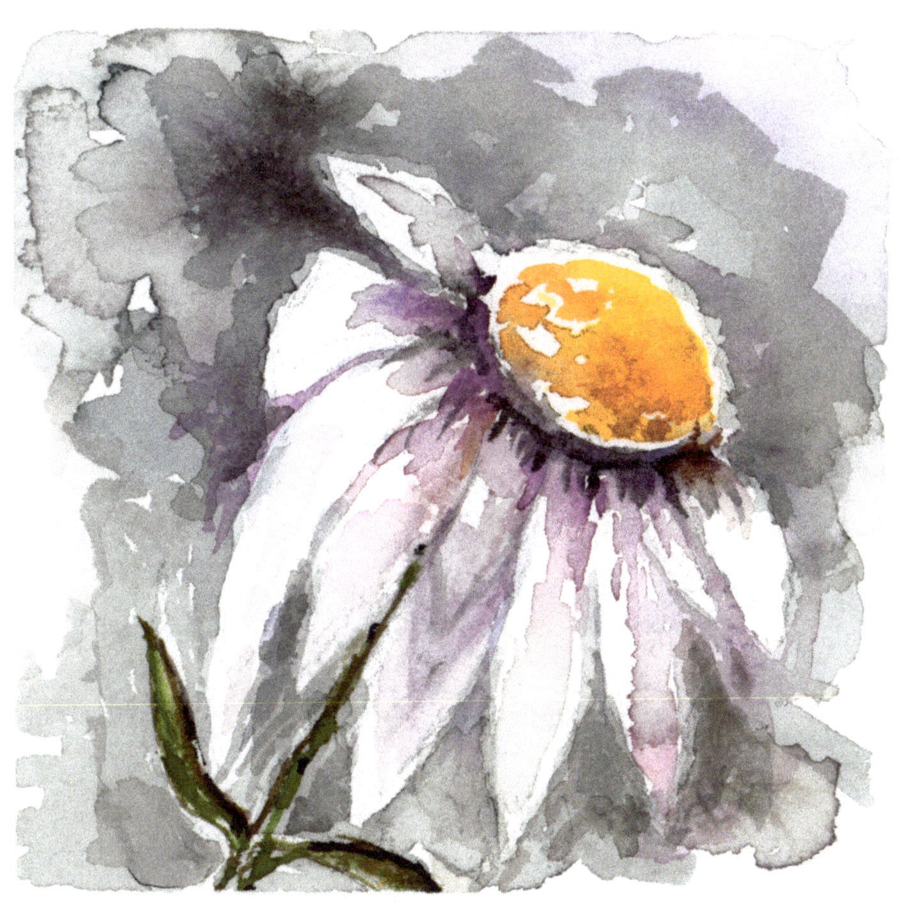

Wednesday

Wednesday is a day for "asynchronistic learning," so everyone stays home and off Zoom. What this means in practice is that students respond when it's convenient. There's no set schedule. They work independently. I choose to sleep in and spend time outdoors with a few friends.

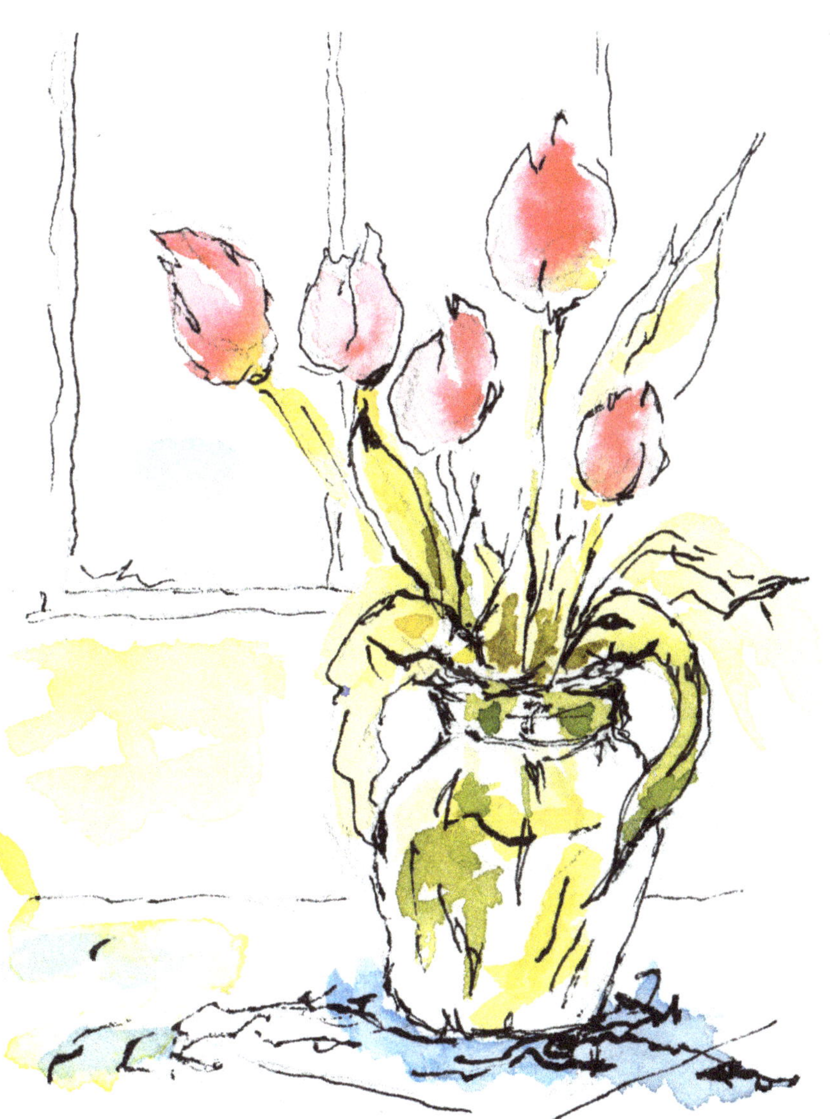

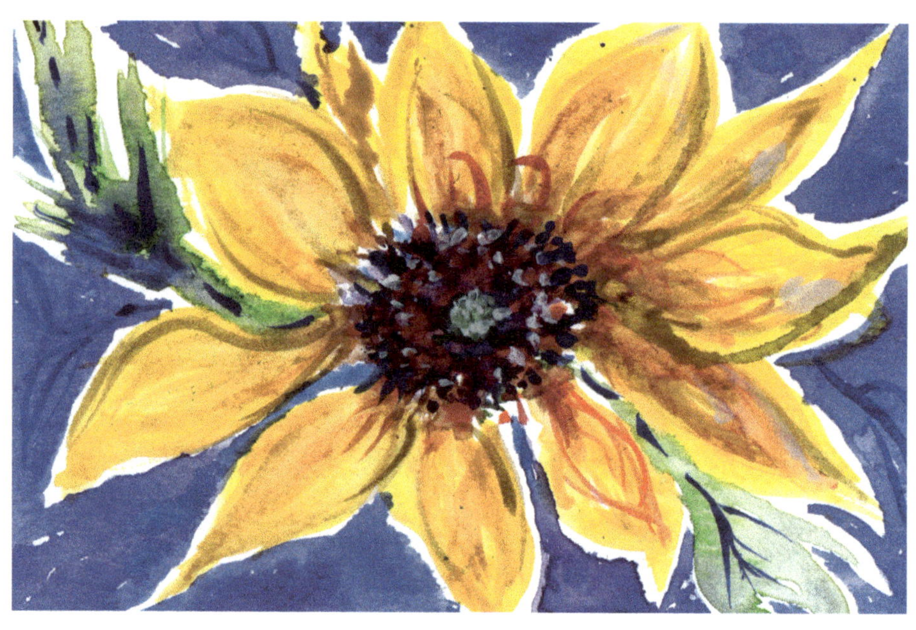

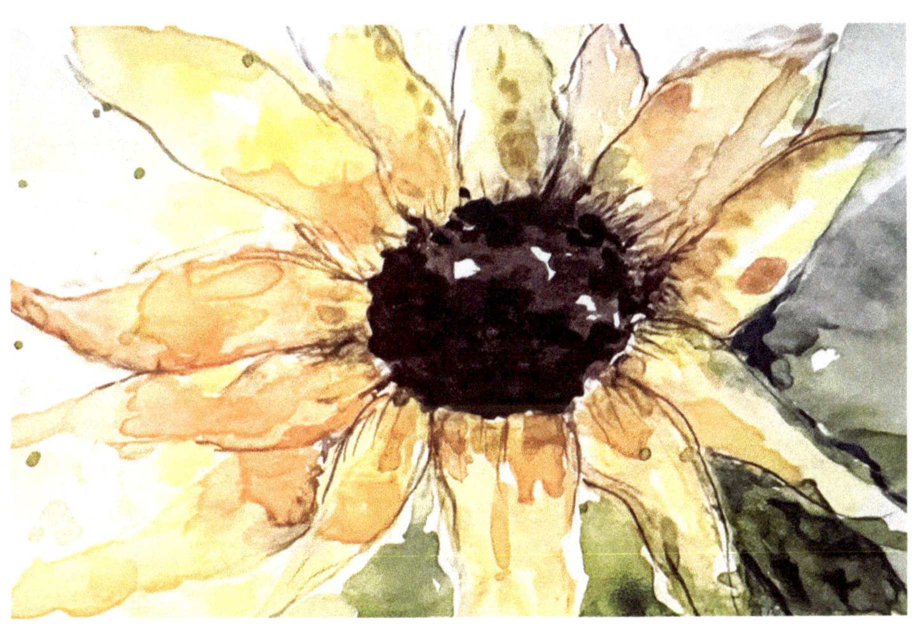

Thursday

I accept a remote assignment for the morning and an in-person assignment for the afternoon, leaving enough time to grab a lunch to go and make the thirty-minute drive. In the morning, I have two kindergarten students named Robert and Ocean.

"Let's count up to one hundred together by fives before we begin class," I say. I ask Robert and Ocean if they would like to start the day with a silly face, a wave, or a smile, or to speak a greeting. I follow instructions and ask them to repeat after me: "I am responsible, respectful, and ready to learn. I follow the group plan. I do my job. I am ready to learn." Robert's face on the camera looks like it's turning green. Then, I realize he's using a green marker to color the camera lens on his school-loaned Chromebook.

"Where is your Thursday folder, Robert?" I ask, attempting to distract him from his antics.

I hear noise in the background as a large woman with rollers in her hair walks by the screen, shouting something. Parents need to pick up "kits" each week from the school to have the supplies needed for the lessons. Mom didn't have a car. Robert has no supplies. I ask him to find a piece of paper and hold it up to the camera. Instead, he holds up his gerbil. Moments later, his camera is off.

Ocean is very patient and earns a few points, but his internet is unstable and his mic doesn't work, so I never hear his voice. I now understand the digital divide, along with many other inequities and challenges laid bare during the Covid-19 pandemic.

In the afternoon, I drive to a middle school I've never been to before, though the name of the school sounds familiar. As I pull into a parking spot, it hits me that I've taught at this school before, but only remotely. After going through the Covid protocols of hand sanitizing, wipes, temperature check, and clean pen to dirty pen sign-in at the office, I don my district fitted and certified N-95 mask and step into the classroom. One of the six third graders who's been on Zoom for the past year but is now sitting in the classroom shouts, "Hey, you look like the lady from my iPad!"

Very few students are in attendance, and there are no pencils or paper—only computers on large, spaced-out tables with charging stations. Each in-person learner is logged on, zeroed in, and playing video learning games. Before I can announce, "Let's go outdoors," a fire alarm sounds a drill and we all jump like we've been stuck with a hot wire. The kids line up robot-like and zombie-walk to the field. I'm suddenly surrounded by a group of twenty-something-year-old teachers, all masked and busy on their cell phones. As they quietly march their troops to their designated zones, I laugh at my "back in my day" thoughts of land phone lines, carbon paper, white-out, and typewriters.

Today, I'm a facilitator of Zoom, chats, breakout rooms, synchronistic learning, asynchronistic learning, password recovery, and the emergent AI normal. Sifting through the ashes of my previous self, I will clear away anything that inhibits creating in this new terrain.

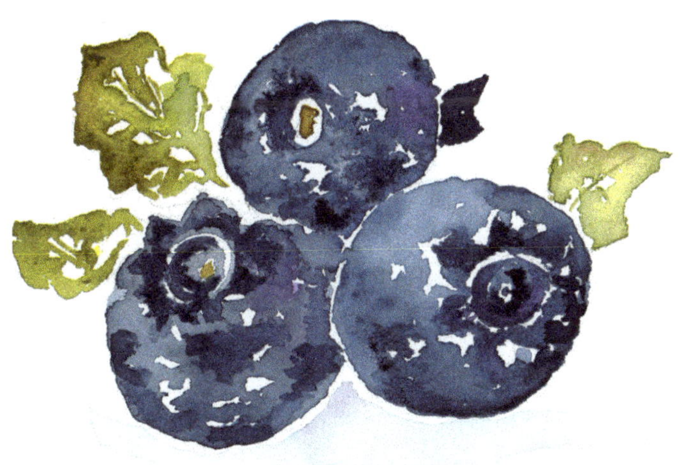

Friday

What teaching assignment might appear for me on this day? I check into the online guest teacher job app on my phone and grab the first one—middle school music. In person. When I was in sixth grade, I played the violin, as did my older sister. My big brother played the trombone, and my kid brother played the trumpet. We proudly took our assigned loaner instruments home, most likely torturing our parents while practicing for concerts and recitals. We had a ton of fun, feeling part of something greater.

After a quick trip down my own personal memory lane and a review of the lesson plan in front of me, I greet the four masked in-person students who enter the music room. My instructions tell me to direct the students to log onto their computers. There's no opportunity to choose an instrument. In fact, there are no musical instruments in sight. The sharing of instruments was eliminated during the pandemic. I'm directed to instruct them to listen to a series of videos about the history of the Moog synthesizer. After a break (they play video games), I have them don headphones and then view more videos teaching them how to create beats by tapping their feet along with GoNoodle tunes. (GoNoodle is an online learning tool.) It's me that's beat. I dismiss the class of four, sanitize the desks, and lock the classroom.

Walking across campus and back to the office, I focus on a beautiful fading rainbow and imagine sauntering along a forest trail, connected by a wonderland of tall trees with strong roots. I'm a teacher and I'm resilient. It's been a difficult road, but educators like me ignite hope and choose to find solutions.

Thank goodness it's Friday.

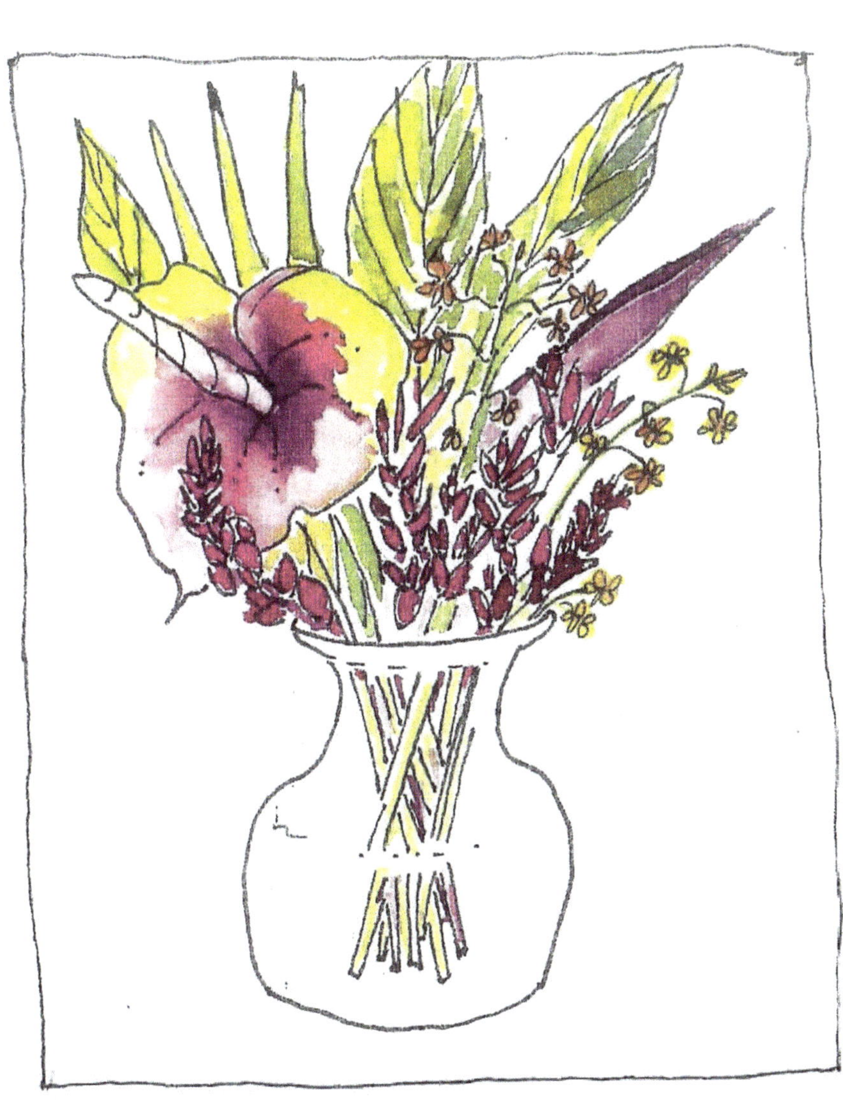

Chapter 11

The Light Was Too Dim

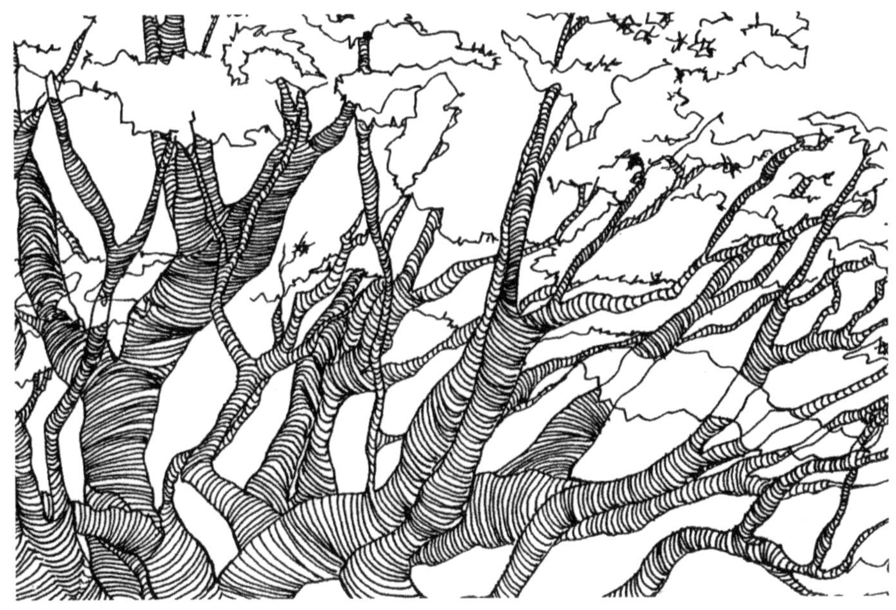

"The light was too dim," Eva replied after I asked why she hadn't done her homework.

As a public school teacher, I was used to all kinds of excuses for why my students didn't have homework to turn in. I expected the familiar story of "my dog ate my homework" or, more recently, "I didn't feel like doing it," but Eva's response left me apprehensive. She went on to explain that the battery had been too low and that the fading dome light in the car made it difficult to read.

• • •

After a lengthy hiatus from teaching, I'd been looking forward to facilitating learning with young people again. I was back from world travels for my travel company and in the Seattle area. At 6 a.m., I heard a buzzing notification on my phone, clicked on an app, and accepted a guest teaching position, one of my few since Covid-19 had shut down schools in 2020. Forgetting that I could work from home, I made the half-hour drive to an empty school. I'd gone through nine digital learning modules to facilitate this new way of doing school, and I was ready to jump in, but in the haste of the morning I'd overlooked that in-person learning was a thing of the recent past—at least for now.

I pulled my car into a deserted lot and parked between two unattended wheeled carts of "free books" and "grab-n-go" meals. This state-of-the-art school had recently undergone a $43 million remodel, but today it was dark and vacant with a skeletal three-person office staff. I hadn't expected to arrive to an abandoned campus. After completing an online health screen outside in a cold drizzle via my cell phone, I masked up, sanitized surfaces and self, and was only then admitted into the secured building and handed a sanitized pen and a sanitized computer from behind a glass screen.

After more than an hour of virtual tech help and several password changes over the phone, I succeeded in logging into the school's computer to meet twenty-three virtual second graders in a Zoom classroom. I attempted to take attendance by the first names that appeared on the screen under their live faces, but they appeared and disappeared as the students logged on and off or disappeared from the screen's view for reasons I couldn't discern.

I felt as though I were teaching with my eyes closed for most of the day. I struggled to make out which of the students were talking, making side conversations, or sending chats. Frustrated, I began to have serious doubts about this style of virtual learning and the entire quality of these students' education.

All but two kids were at home in their bedrooms or their auntie's bedroom. Everyone wanted to give me a tour of their stuff, which I discouraged. It somehow felt invasive and not right. The two other students were at noisy daycare facilities. After a brief self-introduction, I asked the class what they'd done over the weekend.

How do I call on kids? I wondered.

A few kids raised their hands, some with the use of an icon, but most of them talked at once. The answers were similar: I played video games. I watched a movie. I watched TV. No one mentioned going outside. Later that morning, when I suggested they take a stretch break and go outside for some fresh air, they said they weren't allowed to go outside, or that going outside was boring.

Feeling overwhelmed and blue-screen tired, I told everyone to get a book and take a ten-minute reading break. We'd come back together, and they'd share the five W's (who, what, why, when, where) of what they read with the whole class. Three kids said they didn't know how to read English very well. Two kids said they didn't have any books in the house. One kid said he'd been reading a story about the Civil War and asked which side won.

"Was it the Onion?" Hector inquired.

I tried to explain that it was pronounced "U"—Union. But Hector was lost in bouncing up and down on his bed, not listening to an answer to his own question. He did make sure I knew that Miguel was absent because he didn't have internet.

An enthusiastic student named Cyrus, with a cartoon of a cat for his screen face, was reading a sports magazine and shared how some athletes take hemorrhoids to perform better. I suggested that he must mean steroids, but Hannah interrupted. "Don't you know? That painful itching and burning," as if she'd jumped out of a TV commercial. The chats and likes were streaming in like a flooding river, showing up on the bottom of my computer screen. I shuddered at the thought that this day could have been recorded.

Despite my Zoom training through the school district, I found myself to also be click-happy, shifting students from one breakroom to another, popping in and out of breakrooms, and struggling to mute certain disruptive students' mics. (*Is that even allowed?*)

While waiting for the specialists (PE, reading, music, etc.) to show up, I improvised a "name that animal" game by holding up pictures on my cell phone. No specialists showed up. If this had been an in-person class, I would've had supplies for an activity or been able to make a phone call or go down the hall to check on a specialist. Maybe the students were supposed to be reminded to press a red button/link to join a specialist? Instead, I learned about guinea pigs, mom's boyfriend, kittens, dead uncles, and what they had for lunch. Trying to convince Cyrus he shouldn't discipline his "bad" guinea pig because their brains are too small was futile.

I sat, legs cramping, for four hours making up word and math games. None of the kids wanted to take a break or log off at the end of the day because they were home alone and didn't want to be offline and alone. Personally, I was craving outdoor time. Feeling somewhat guilty, and completely exhausted, I said goodbye to the class with a click.

As I packed up to leave my deserted borrowed classroom, I wondered how students without a home, like Eva, or without the internet, like Miguel, would receive a decent education in this digital world. Will students after the X, Y, Z, and Alpha generations, born after 2013, be considered a repeat of the L, or Lost, Generation of 1890? Or, having never known a world before smart phones, perhaps this emerging digital Gen Alpha is precisely on track to becoming the well-educated, diverse, entrepreneurial, and most connected generation ever. Or maybe AI will surpass or own us all.

I pulled up my N95 mask to pass by the office and crept out to the parking lot, lost in thoughts about this generation. I considered the possibility that the Covid era was reshaping the political, social, and economic landscape, and that the gamification of learning was creating a generation with impaired social formations, eyesight problems, and shorter attention spans. Would these emerging divergent thinkers also be facing a dangerous disconnect from nature?

It occurred to me that I could be the lost one—lost in digital incompetence and stuck in an old-school baby boomer mindset. After all, I don't have my own YouTube channel—nor a TikTok username—and I don't know how to make one.

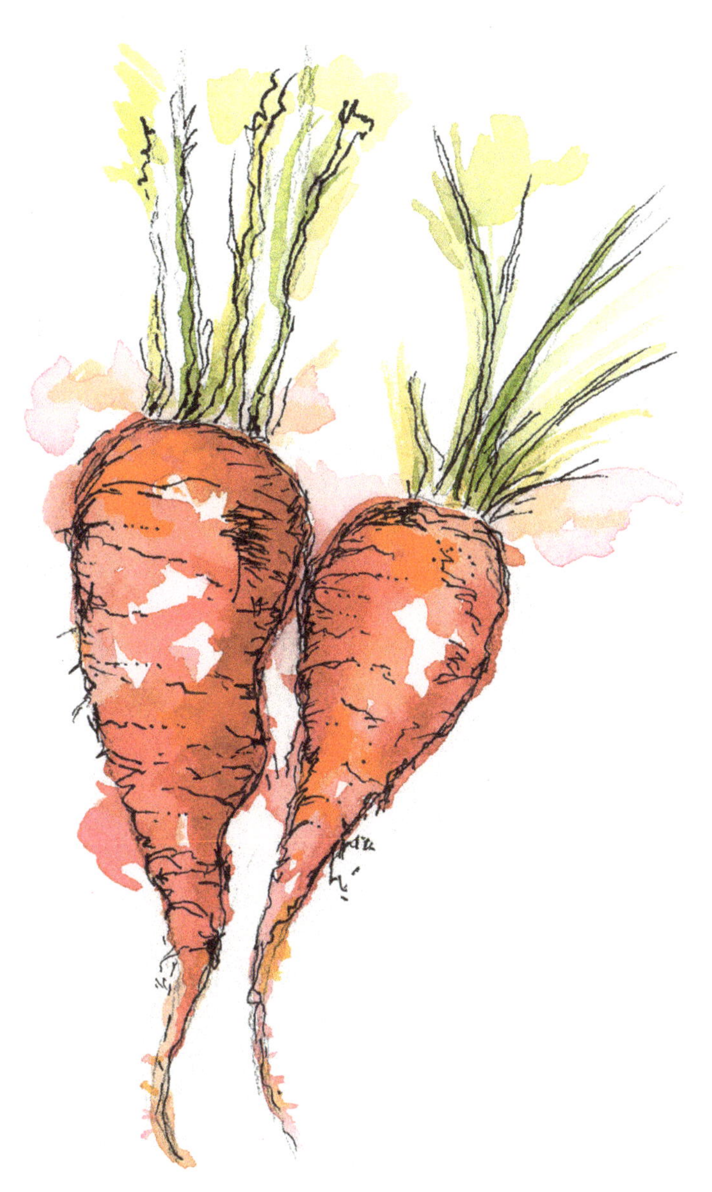

Chapter 12

Quarantine Bliss

ACCORDING TO THE BEAST

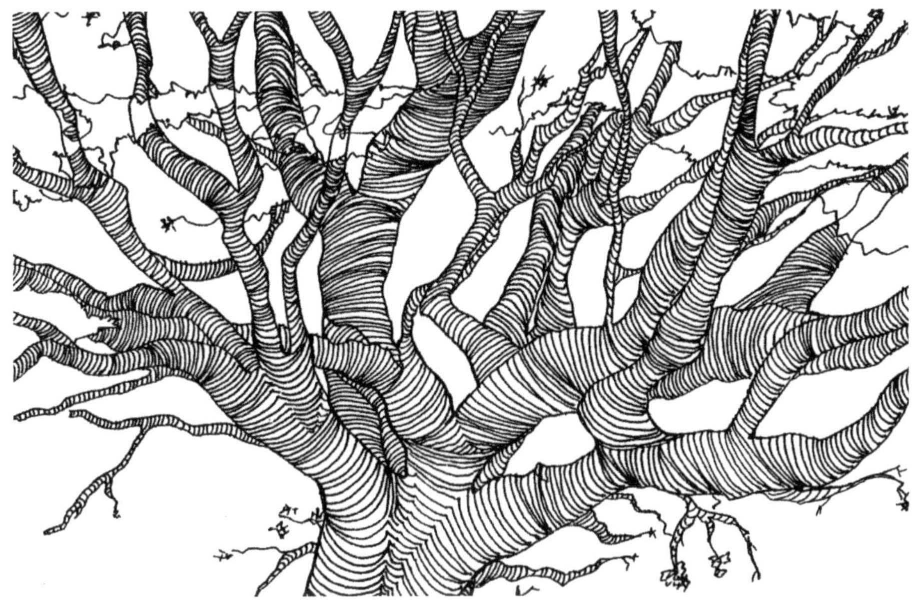

To some humans, staying home during a global pandemic is as harsh as lockdown prison, filled with sadness, fear, anger, lost jobs, lost community, lost security, and lost lives. But for a cat like me, the silver linings are bountiful now that I'm not out prowling for goldfinches. I'm appreciated, finally, as good company and talked to more than my feline pals ever spoke to me. During the short commute from her bed to her home office, Island Jane delivers a tremendous amount of petting—between her excessive handwashing and sanitizing, that is.

As I blissfully sprawl across a sheepskin before the fireplace, I ponder how proud I am to be the owner of Island Jane and Doer Doug. Not only do they listen to me now that we're quarantined together, but they mimic me with their frequent catnapping, constant snacking, and be-here-now behavior.

When Island Jane isn't catnapping, I observe the many hours she spends at her computer from my spot on her lap. Together, we marvel for long hours at the tiny water droplets making their way down the exterior of the shuttered bedroom window to merge with bigger droplets. Transfixed, we follow the trail of an iridescent green beetle and watch it dig a perfectly round hole in the soil of a windowsill herb pot.

It hasn't always been easy being a cat. My earliest memories are far from purrfect. I was only a kitten when my siblings and I were thrown out of a moving car. My littermates scattered, leaving me to fend for myself with a shattered leg in the jungles of Hawai'i's Big Island. I tried to be tough like a wild animal, but all I could do was cry. My desperate pleas for help were loud and persistent and eventually answered by a kind old woman. Crouching down from her rickety stance, she lifted my scrawny, injured frame from the bottom of the long dirt driveway and took me into her home. She bombarded me with toys and tasty treats but wouldn't let me explore. I was as restless as a willow in a storm and as neurotic as a bee without a hive.

I tried to run away once, but my timing was bad. The sudden eruption of Mount Kilauea filled every path with danger and lava flows that swallowed forests and houses. Somehow, I found my way back to the old woman's house, preferring safety, inactivity, and boredom to dodging scorched earth and rivers of fire. But the woman's life shifted during this drawn-out and unpredictable disaster. She reluctantly handed me off to Jungle Jane and Doer Doug, who moved us to Seattle to escape the spewing volcano. For me, that meant confinement in a crate on a very long solo flight over the Pacific. Not that I know what the Pacific is.

We moved into a van next, bouncing around from town to town, on and off slow and fast roads, searching for a home without wheels. I didn't like van life any more than I liked the earthquakes, confinement, and mongooses of Hawai'i. The vinyl seats were un-cozy and scratchy to sleep on, and the stale air of the van reminded me of a neglected litter box. Anytime the van slowed or stopped, everything shifted forward. Inevitably, something broke or spilled, usually on me.

By the time we found a home on a tiny island south of a place they called Seattle, Island Jane and Doer Doug started talking about a virus that was taking over the world and killing lots of humans. I don't know what that had to do with cats—we weren't dying—but quarantine was announced, and none of us was allowed to leave home. I wasn't happy about it at first, but this new state of house arrest turned out to be heaven for a wounded critter like me. I've never been more paw-licking satisfied. I find myself on a peaceful island in Washington State, free to chase an abundance of gnawers and deer in between all the catnapping.

There are no hard and fast routines. Flitting birds, retractable claw stretches, and addictive cat treats fill my days. Days pass with no obligations or plans. Island Jane and I have gone for long walks together—which, by the way, is unusual for a distracted cat. It seems we now go in and out of the house together as a family, which works for me. I surprise myself with a soft purr now and then. I feel a new sense of belonging with and tail-twitching appreciation for Island Jane and Doer Doug. I like bringing them furry gifts—both dead and alive. And I have freedom of movement. No more van!

I'm finally OK with my bum foot, which I accept as part of my wild journey. The beastly days of biting and attacking for no reason are behind me. I've made my peace with hairballs and bugs. I never have known what tomorrow would bring, but now I accept that all things change. In the blissful era of Covid quarantine, this happy beast is as content as she'll ever be. We've all learned to slow down and appreciate each other, and that's enough.

I still wonder, though—why do they call me The Beast?

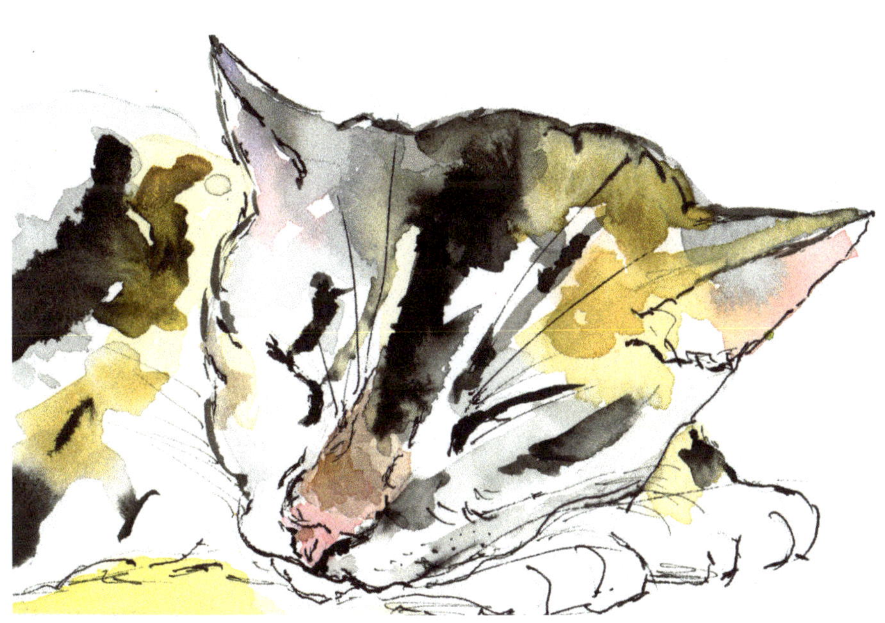

Chapter 13

Nothing and Everything

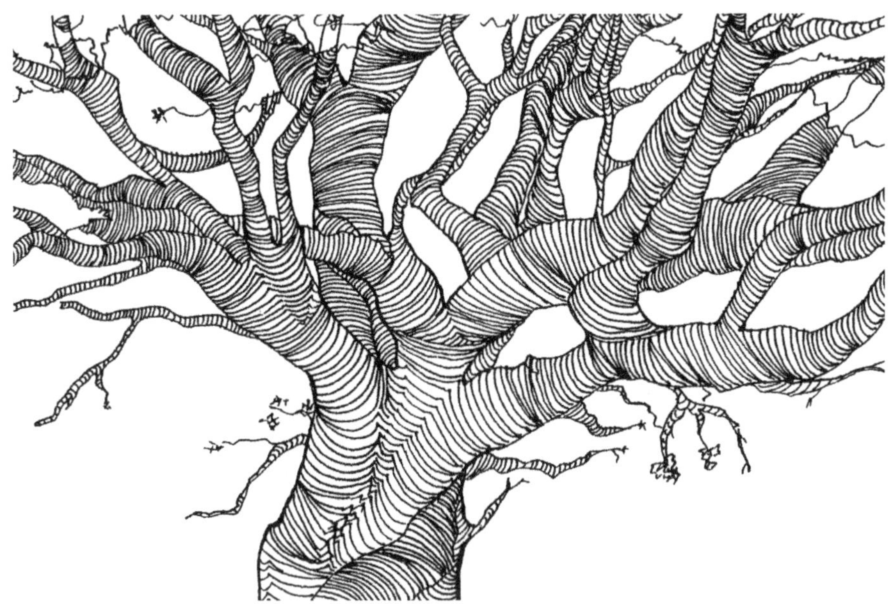

This is a story about nothing. And everything.

A turning point.

It's been more than a year and it's a time to reinvent. I start the day feeling zombie-like. I desperately need a walk in the woods to refresh. I set out on a quiet trail in a mossy wood under a darkening sky that's reflective of my mood. I feel numb, blank, stuck on rock bottom. My thoughts wind around unfulfilled expectations. Around a vast nothingness.

As I walk in the stillness, I'm struck with a fearful sensation of that nothingness. To me, "nothing" is the absence of what I expect to be there or to happen. "Nothing" is a void, like when I have nothing to say, or when I draw a blank, or when I'm unable to think of anything to think about.

I remember a time when, feeling broken after ending a passionate relationship, I bushwhacked deep into the wild edges of an Alaskan wilderness. The recollection causes my mind to close in on absence, vacancy, and abandonment. For a fleeting moment, I recall another time when I dived into the dark depths of the Blue Hole in Belize, expecting something, only to experience nothingness in space and time. A dark void.

Nothingness is being shut down and stuck on empty. Nothing is having no single thing of value nor trace of any order. Nothing means not anything. Nothing is a feeling of nonexistence, of being breathless with a stuck pause button and a closed heart. Nothing is perhaps what I will feel when I pass through the thin veil that separates the living from the dead.

I continue my walk down the soggy, deserted trail to nowhere. I continue to feel nothing, the opposite of mindfulness. Meaningless. I consider giving up on the regular order of life. Nothing from nothing—that matches my empty feeling.

But, if I'm truthful, I'm no more capable of turning off the din of life than I am of quitting the desire for order, peace, and grace in both my inner and outer worlds. I do want and expect something. Deterioration, succumbing like the decomposing leaves underfoot, is not an option for me. Not yet anyway. *No, you aren't lost*, I assure myself. *You belong. You are fortunate.*

I slow my pace to lean into the dripping forest, to slough off the residue from the never-ending drone of planes, cars, friction on pavement. The urban cacophony that occupies and gnaws at my entire being every day in the city begins to dissolve. I notice an inner shift occurring in the new silence. A heightened sensation, a feeling of lightening, overwhelms me as I spring to new ground. Allowing myself to feel liberated amongst the towering cedars and firs, I inhale and exhale deeply and began to fill my well.

People who have nothing always desire something. Perhaps they want food, shelter, love. They want dreams to come true or they want to invite trouble. We all want nothing, or we want something, but we want. At this precise moment, all I want is right in front of me. Time has slowed. Each step I place on the soggy path, each breath I take, squeezes out a new truth. I appreciate my existence.

All around me, the tiniest of natural sounds collaborate to form a symphony that awakens my spirit. I listen keenly to the loud silence, becoming attuned to the wonder of several duck's feet paddling through a small pond. The whoosh of bird's wings overhead. The snap of a twig as a squirrel bounds for cover. I imagine I hear worms eating dirt. I sense nematodes and fungi gripping and grinding soil as they move their circular muscles through sinuous underground tunnels. I feast on the mystery.

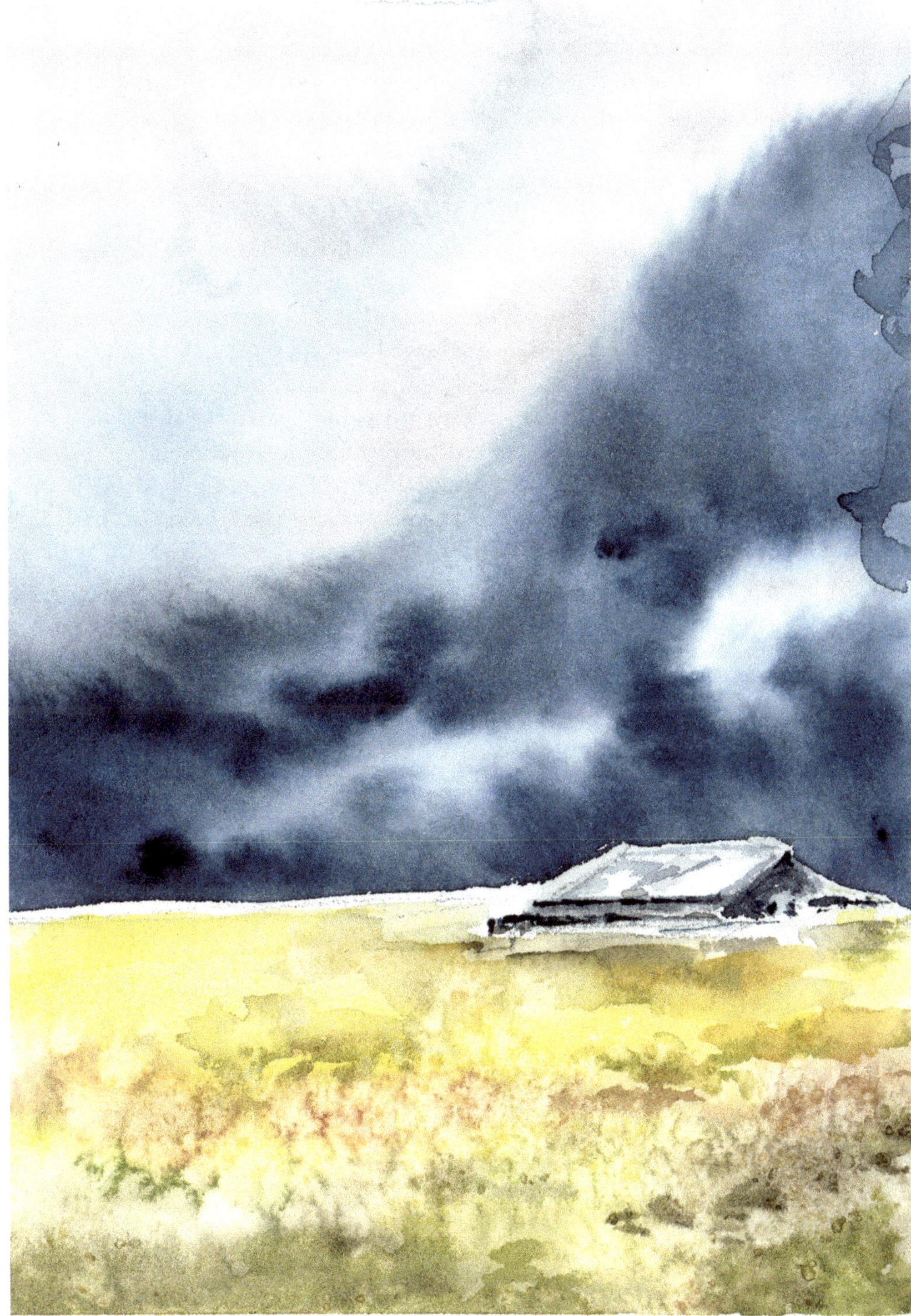

As the rain showers slow and the sky begins to lighten, I choose the correct turn on the muddy path and end up looping back into full sunlight. It's no surprise I've made a complete circle. There, at the trail's end, I inhale loudly, and with an open mind and a fresh laugh I emit an unusually throaty "Woo- hoo!"

At the start of this walk, I felt buried, crushed, lost beneath a dark, low-hanging cloud of doubt and disbelief. My very bones had been rattled, smacked and stunned by racing thoughts of escalating chaos, disgrace, and disease in the world. Unbelievable for someone who's default is positivity? No. I'm human, after all. My precious well-being had been dislodged. But at this turnaround moment, I honor myself and the privilege of being alive. Struck by a renewed spark, I once again awaken to the magic and wonder of life. I'm heated up and ready for pouring, like one of those electric teakettles that turns blue when the water begins to boil. I feel ignited and primed for infinite possibilities.

One overflowing and scalding epiphany after another hits me as I reach out to grip my car door handle. All I wanted was to see nothing but the truth. I purposely put myself in the forest today to hear it, see it, feel it, and taste it. With reawakened clarity and peace of mind, I sense my spirit is newly able to connect with my highest purpose.

I'm reminded that focusing on personal and infinite truth takes imagination, belief in positive outcomes, internal exploration, and buckets of courage. A simple walk in the woods has turned out to be immensely restorative and joyous. And it put me in a refreshing place of renewal. I'm about to turn a page on a new chapter of my life. I cannot control external things, but I can choose to control me. Nothing, I tell myself, is going to keep me from my own inner council. I choose to invite abundant possibilities and author the book of something.

Today, nothing became everything.

And tomorrow, this is what will get me up in the morning, as it does all mornings: Creating Things, Seeing Possibilities, Starting Things, Making Connections, Empowering Others.

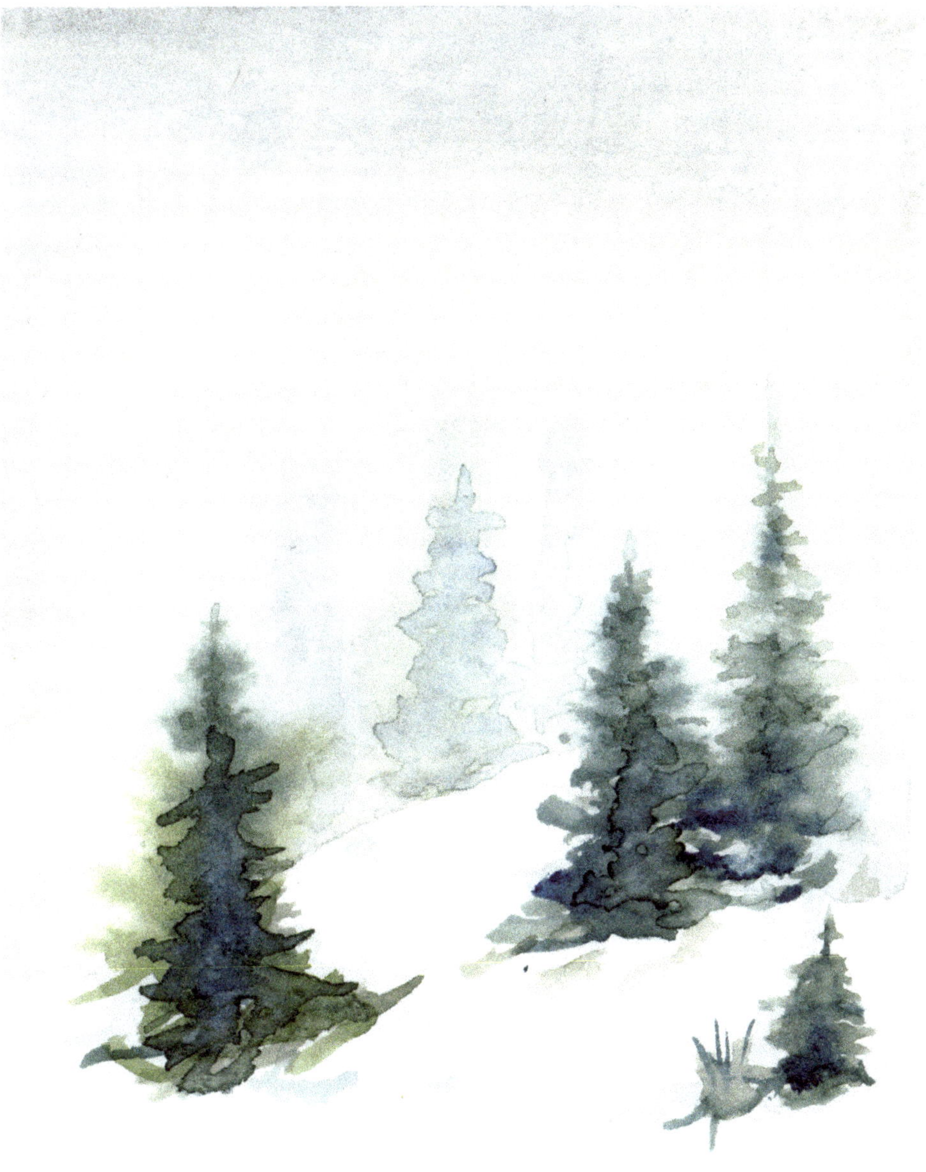

EPILOGUE

What will your next chapter look like?

As a trained Purpose Workshop Facilitator for the Blue Zones Wellness Project, I often asked workshop participants—teachers, businesspeople, senior residents, and students of all ages—to try this exercise on life: Take a tape measure and pull it out. Find the number that matches your current age and mark that number with a piece of tape. Then, make an educated guess how long you think you will live and mark that number. Now, look at how much or how little time you have left between your two marks.

What joy will you create today? How will you choose to use your gifts and talents?

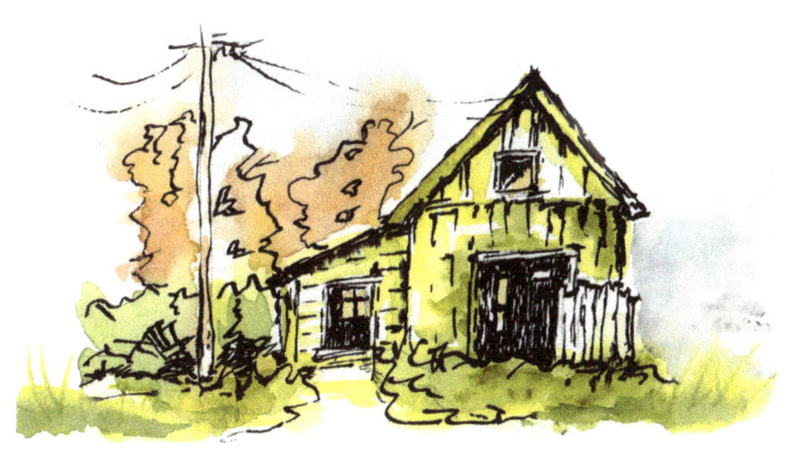

ACKNOWLEDGMENTS

Big hugs and extreme thanks to my partners, my two "kids" Tyler and Olivia, my four sibs, and my wide-ranging network of family and friends.

Remembering my loving parents who instilled a lifelong love of nature in me. The pen and ink drawings throughout this book are my interpretations of a live oak tree that still grows strong at their former home, Sunny Ridge Farm, in Winters, California.

Expressing gratitude for all the questions, collaboration, and constructive feedback I received in writing and painting classes.

Recognizing dear friends and lifelong mentors who continue to provide encouragement along this creative journey.

Appreciating all the young people I've worked with in creating purpose.

Feeling fortunate to have collaborated with Demitasse Press co-founders Sara Roahen and Dorka Hegedus in making the editing and publishing of this collection of life stories possible.

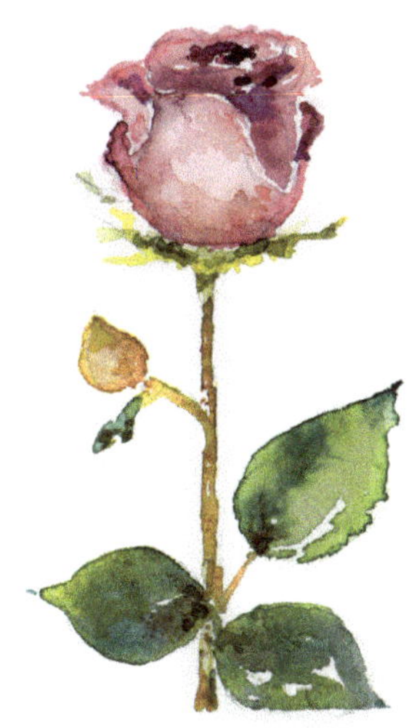

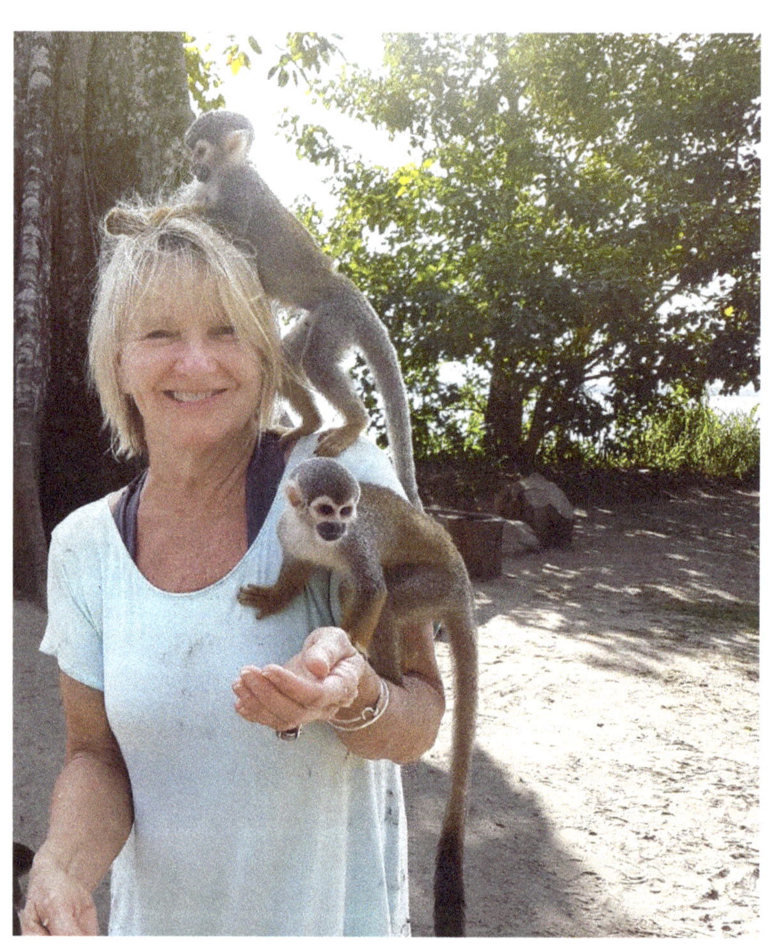

ABOUT THE AUTHOR

Jane Howard is a teacher, artist, naturalist guide, mother, entrepreneur, and adventurer known for gravitating to and living on islands. She earned her nickname Island Jane while pioneering ecotourism in the San Juan Islands in the Pacific Northwest. For more than a decade, Jane conducted nature-based learning experiences from a former hunting lodge on a remote private island. Through the Pacific Science Center and her company Island Institute, mud mucking in tide flats and cold water plunging became integral parts of her total immersion experiences. Jane is at home snorkeling in fifty-degree water and recording observations of orca and minke whales from her kayak.

Relocating to the US Virgin Islands, Jane facilitated fun science challenges for youth in and on the water. After falling in love with tropical environments, she moved to the Big Island, Hawai'i, to design place-based curricula for Kamehameha Schools and to conduct engaging learning experiences for students in Hawaiian immersion schools. With the support of the Seattle-based Adventure Travel Trade Association, Jane created business-to-business events in Hawai'i, connecting diverse adventure operators while promoting cultural and natural history interpretation. Before the eruption of Kilauea in 2018, which buried her home and belongings in more than forty feet of lava, Jane introduced hundreds of individuals to the magic flow of the lush and active Hawaiian Islands.

Lured back to the Pacific Northwest, Jane now finds her happy place on a tiny private island in South Puget Sound, Washington, where she enjoys messing about with painting adventures and other creative projects. She describes her two amazing children, also thriving on the West Coast, as "outstanding natural wonders."

Broadening her reach, Jane co-created Girls on the Go Destinations in 2020, a global travel company with the mission of bringing small groups of dynamic women together to travel the globe and connect with fabulous locals in fascinating places. After selling the business, she reinvented collaborative travel experiences through her new company, Island Jane Journeys. www.islandjanejourneys.com

Jane has guided curious individuals and groups in steamy jungles, to remote beaches, and, naturally, on islands, collaborating with diverse organizations that include: the Smithsonian Associates Travel Program, The Pacific Science Center, Bill Nye the Science Guy, National Geo Kids, Jungle to Table events, EF Tours, Eco Teach, Happy By Design, Island Institute, Islandjane Ecotours, Islandjane Journeys, Girls on the Go Destinations, International Wildlife Adventures, Western Washington University, The University of Washington, The National Association of Interpretive Naturalists, and the National Audubon Society.

Jane is a licensed Master Educator and certified Interpretive Naturalist Guide, and she's been recognized by *Outside Magazine*'s Travel Hub Award. Her essays have been published in *Clearing Magazine* and *The Planet*, Western Washington University College for the Environment's magazine.

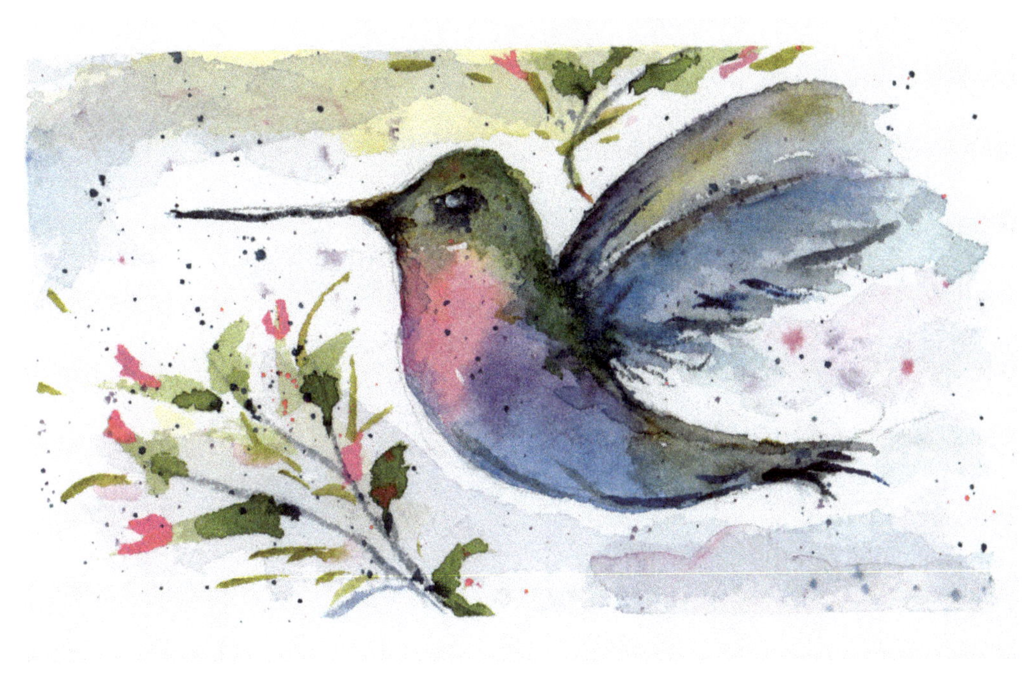

BIO OF THE BEAST

Island Jane took some serious training. She was as busy as a hummingbird until I domesticated her and taught her to slow down and behave. The boss is the one with the tail, and I'm a special cat. I've always had a full agenda of doing nothing. Despite the many interruptions and changes to my journey, I now pride myself in having complete control of my very own pet, Island Jane, who caters to my every desire.

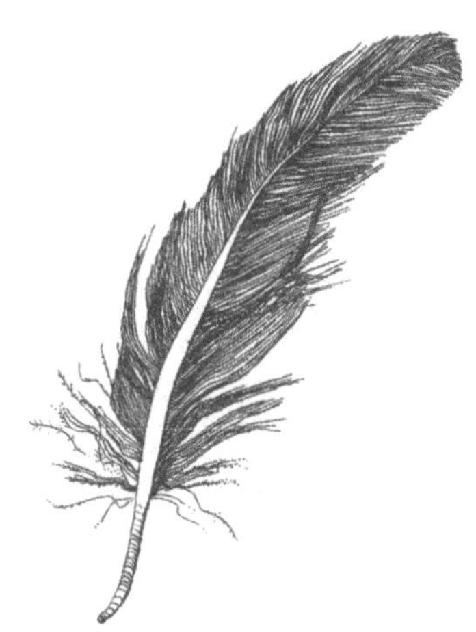

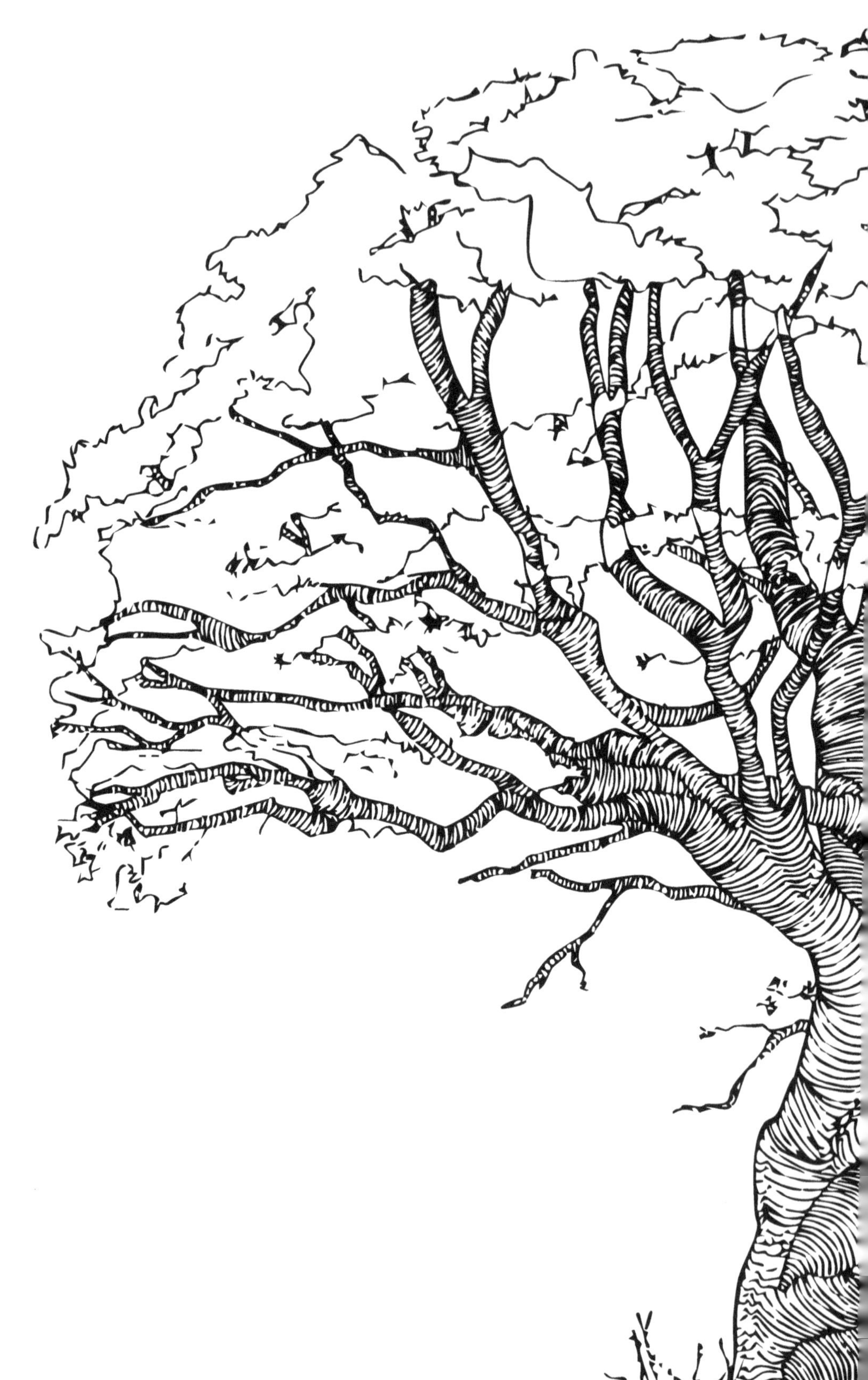

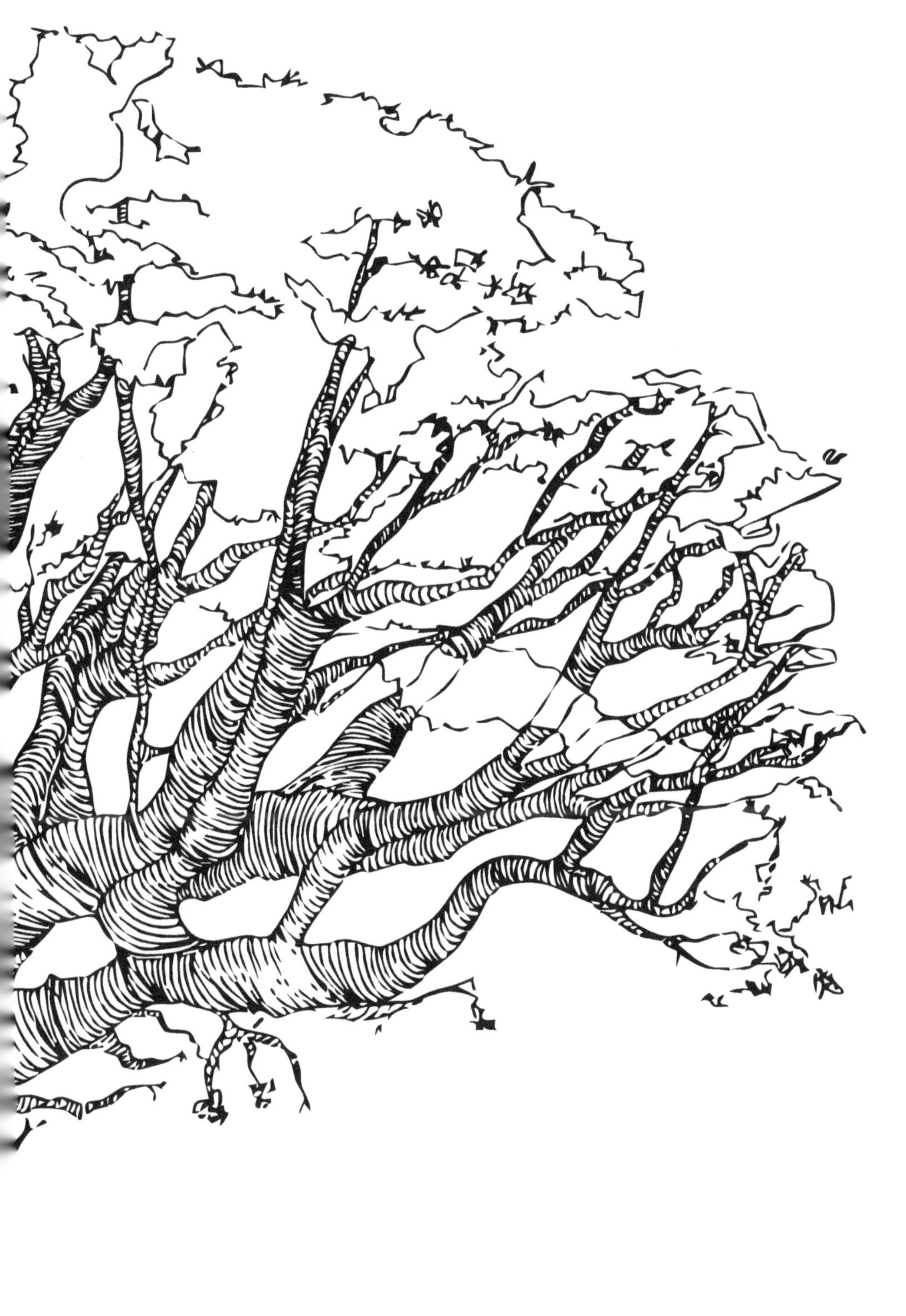

www.ingramcontent.com/pod-product-compliance
Lightning Source LLC
LaVergne TN
LVHW051939100826
845155LV00013B/28/J

* 9 7 9 8 9 9 2 9 9 7 4 3 9 *